Developing Good Practice in Community Care

of related interest

Community Care Practice and the Law
Second Edition
Michael Mandelstam
ISBN 1 85302 647 6

Competence in Social Work Practice
A Practical Guide for Professionals
Edited by Kieran O'Hagan
ISBN 1 85302 332 9

Cultural Competence in the Caring Professions
Kieran O'Hagan
ISBN 1 85302 759 6

Research in Social Care and Social Welfare
Issues and Debates for Practice
Edited by Beth Humphries
ISBN 1 85302 900 9

Handbook of Theory for Practice Teachers in Social Work
Edited by Joyce Lishman
ISBN 1 85302 098 2

Social Workers, the Community and Social Interaction
Intervention and the Sociology of Welfare
John Offer
ISBN 1 85302 731 6

The Changing Role of Social Care
Edited by Bob Hudson
ISBN 1 85302 752 9

Planning and Costing Community Care
Edited by Chris Clark and Irvine Lapsley
ISBN 1 85302 267 5

Developing Good Practice in Community Care

Partnership and Participation

Edited by
Vicky White and John Harris

Jessica Kingsley Publishers
London and Philadelphia

The right of the contributors to be identified as authors of this work has been asserted by them in accordance with the Copyright, Designs and Patents Act 1988.

First published in the United Kingdom in 2001 by
Jessica Kingsley Publishers Ltd,
116 Pentonville Road, London
N1 9JB, England
and
325 Chestnut Street,
Philadelphia PA 19106, USA.

www.jkp.com

Library of Congress Cataloging in Publication Data
A CIP catalog record for this book is available from the Library of Congress

British Library Cataloguing in Publication Data
A CIP catalogue record for this book is available from the British Library

ISBN 1 85302 890 8

Printed and Bound in Great Britain by
Athenaeum Press, Gateshead, Tyne and Wear

CONTENTS

Acknowledgements

Our thanks go to Chris Hallett for spotting the potential for the project, out of which this book emerged, from the moment it first surfaced in a chance meeting in a sandwich shop; to David Mason, previous Director of Social Services in Warwickshire, for embracing it enthusiastically; to Trish Haines, current Director of Social Services, for her continued support; and to those contributors to the project who were unable to engage in producing the book, for a variety of reasons: Janet Barnett, Denise Cross, Jo Johnson, Alex Killeen, Gwen Norrie, Renée Pennington, and Sue Wensley.

Most importantly, we extend heartfelt thanks to the participants in the project who volunteered to try their hands at being authors. They have worked long and hard to see the book realised. Our other contributors receive similar thanks. The positive attitude of all of you to our interventions in your work has made the task of editing the book much more pleasant then it might otherwise have been.

Preface

This book arises from the aftermath of one of the biggest upheavals to have taken place in the history of social work: the reform of community care. It emerged from a project in Warwickshire Social Services Department which set out to identify examples of good practice in the context of the profound changes which have occurred since the implementation of the National Health Service and Community Care Act (1990).

Being willing to engage the social services department in the project was a typically bold decision on the part of the then Director, David Mason. It was bold because it was an act of faith, in four ways. First, it assumed that good practice was waiting to be uncovered within the department. Second, it envisaged staff being able to grasp the opportunity of standing back from the changed and changing terrain in which they worked, and then using their individual and collective experiences from the vantage points afforded by their particular locations in the department. Third, it held that it was possible for social work to adapt to the changes in community care without shedding its commitment to problem-solving in partnership with people in the community. This was an overall approach which had been endorsed by Warwickshire County Council, in stark contrast to the tick-box mentality of many other social services departments' implementation of the community care reforms (Barnes 1997, p.139). This problem-solving in partnership approach has since been identified as the basis from which social work might be reinvented and realigned with contemporary societal conditions (Smale, Tuson and Statham 2000, p.13). Fourth, value was placed on the 'front-line culture' in the department. The project was seen as an opportunity for dialogue between that culture and senior managers and politicians.

This act of faith was justified subsequently when staff proved well able to gauge the changes which had taken and were taking place. Participants in the project explored the possibilities those changes contained for the development of good practice in direct work with service users and carers and in strategic thinking. The project demonstrated the ability of practitioners and front-line managers to generate their own reflective analysis of professional practice and organisational strategy. This ability became a tool for staff development through its use in a series of seminar presentations. Examples of good practice were surfaced and presented by project participants to colleagues from across the social services department. Most of the chapters in the book have emerged from those presentations. They were the culmination, at a particular point in time, of a process of self-generated learning which occurred in an organisational context that was open to critical reflection and dialogue.

It will have become apparent that although this is a contemporary book, it is in one sense an unfashionable book. Since the advent of the community care reforms, the prevailing discourse has been managerial. Senior managers have enjoyed a privileged position in conveying their accounts and analyses. Against that managerial backcloth, service user groups have developed their own discourses and have struggled hard to make them heard. Missing, to a great extent, from the ensuing debates have been the voices of social workers and front-line managers. Often they have been left commenting hesitantly from the sidelines. While wanting to endorse emphatically the importance of service users' experiences and accounts (especially given that Warwickshire Social Services Department was committed to their importance *before* the community care reforms were implemented (see, for example, Baldwin *et al.* (1993)), the book begins from the premise that social workers and front-line managers also have contributions to make.

There are signs that central government shares this premise. 'A Quality Strategy for Social Care' (Department of Health 2000d) contains three paragraphs which echo the sentiments which lie behind the process which produced this book:

> 'Social work has a specific contribution to make…with its emphasis on rights and responsibilities, citizenship and participation.' (para. 101).

> 'Staff who deliver services are … a vital source of information about what works and what does not. Their evaluations, from what happens in practice, must be central to service improvements, to spreading good practice and to developing the knowledge base for social care.' (para. 76)

> 'Modern public services value their staff, are open to innovative ideas generated by them and act on those ideas. A culture that resists its workforce's attempts to innovate, or that stifles creativity, is no longer acceptable.' (para. 79)

The book is intended for use not just by social workers and front-line managers but also by students. Given that it is grounded in practice it can be used on qualifying social work programmes in courses concerned with social work strategies and skills, whether such courses address social work in general or are more specifically focused on community care settings. The book can also be used at qualifying level to underpin the placement curriculum, as the issues raised in it will be encountered by social work students when they are being assessed in practice. Beyond the qualifying level, the book provides pointers to the types of material which could be developed by experienced social workers who are submitting portfolios in connection with the Post Qualifying or Advanced Awards. The practice content of the book lends itself to being adapted to the particular emphases and perspectives used in teaching and learning at these different levels. While the beginning social worker might use some of the chapters as templates for practice possibilities in particular placement settings, more experienced practitioners might consider themselves as already operating at a level on a par with the material and might use it more independently as a resource to stimulate their thinking about their own practice.

Whether used at qualifying, post qualifying or advanced levels, the book's title deliberately emphasises 'developing good practice'. 'Developing' signifies that the book is in no sense the final word on any of the topics discussed. 'Good practice' implies that the practice described is considered to have value but does not purport to be perfect practice. As such, the contributors' conceptions and accounts of developing good practice are not final destinations. They are points of departure for debates about the directions in which community care needs to travel. 'Partnership and participation' are significant signposts for that journey, but the precise route to be taken will often be debated heatedly among the range of travellers (service users, carers, managers and practitioners) in community care. The book is simply one set of contributions to that debate.

Chapter One

Changing Community Care

Vicky White and John Harris

Introduction

Social workers and front-line managers in the field of community care have lived through a gale of change over the last ten years. This book is a response to their experiences and is concerned with 'changing community care' in three senses. First, 'changing community care' is simply a statement of fact. Community care has been, and is, changing rapidly. All of the contributors to the book have been caught up in the impact of the changes taking place. Second, 'changing community care' not only is a statement of fact, but also has become an increasingly urgent imperative for social workers and front-line managers who have been involved in the intricate responsibilities of seeing through a range of changes. Third, 'changing community care' suggests that community care can be changed. It enjoins social workers and front-line managers to engage with agendas for change reflectively and pro-actively, taking part in the construction of those agendas, rather than being simply passive recipients of their outcomes.

In the face of 'changing community care', it is easy for social services staff to feel under siege. Report after report has scrutinised their performance and exhorted them to greater efforts in rising to new performance challenges. Service user groups' criticisms and press onslaughts have added to the potential for uncertainty and insecurity, exacerbated by the blurring of their roles with those of other professionals, which is an increasingly characteris-tic feature of their everyday work. In this context some social workers and front-line managers have expressed scepticism about the changes they have experienced and concern for the survival of the ideals and principles which originally attracted them to community care.

This opening chapter sets personal experiences such as these in context. It begins by outlining the changes which have taken place and summarises the implications of three inter-related developments in the community care reforms (marketisation, managerialism and consumerism) for front-line staff.

It moves on to consider the continuities and shifts associated with New Labour's 'Third Way' and concludes with the identification of the progressive potential of partnership and participation.

All change!

The National Health Service and Community Care Act (1990) arguably marked the most significant moment thus far in the development of community care policy and practice. It transformed 'community care' from a vague and disparate aspiration into a specific policy direction and a distinctive set of practices. When the Act was implemented, many workers felt uneasy about what the new-look community care represented. It appeared to be a retreat from the principles according to which social work and the personal social services had been incorporated into the post-war welfare state. Those principles, which drove the establishment of social services departments in the early 1970s, concerned the moral and organisational superiority and desirability of the state delivering service provision which the market did not, and should not, provide. The principles were encapsulated in the report which led to the setting up of social services departments. The Seebohm Report called for 'a community-based and family-oriented service, which would be available to all. This new Department will, we believe, reach far beyond the discovery and rescue of social casualties; it will enable the greatest possible number of individuals to act reciprocally' (Seebohm Report 1968, para. 2). In the reform of community care, this idealistic vision of what social services might achieve through the agency of the state was transformed by four developments which were central to Thatcherite reforms across a range of policy areas: the introduction of market mechanisms; the promotion of competition in the search for efficiency gains and savings; the keeping of state provision to a minimum; the pursuit of individualism and individual choice (Flynn 1993, pp.14–15).

After the 1987 election, attempts over the previous eight years by the Thatcher governments to shape social services policy by the use of financial control were augmented by a radical legislative programme to limit expenditure, break up public provision, increase the scope of commercial sector operations, bring in business management principles to what remained of the public sector and reduce the power of professionals (Jones 1994, p.190 and p.205). The Conservative government's previous reliance on attempting to limit local government spending was replaced by a market-oriented strategy presented as returning control of social services to their users. This post-1987 programme involved fundamental changes in the arrangements for community care which were described by the Audit Commission as 'revolutionary' (Audit Commission 1992a, p.1).

The Audit Commission's report followed considerable impetus for a change of direction for community care found in a number of influential reports in the late 1980s (for example, Audit Commission (1986); Griffiths Report (1988); House of Commons Social Services Committee (1985); Wagner Report (1988); Department of Health (1989)), culminating in the National Health Service and Community Care Act (1990). At a general level, the promotion of a new policy direction in community care, embodying a new legislative and 'market' framework, was integral to the Conservative government's radical project of welfare state reform. However, the immediate incentive to reform community care was economic. It was only when community care was linked to ways of reducing public expenditure that far-reaching change was initiated.

A specific crisis arose through the desire to reduce public expenditure on commercially provided residential care, following a massive increase in social security payments to support residents in private sector residential and nursing homes. Under arrangements introduced by the Conservative government in 1980, the social security system paid the board and lodging costs of people with assets of under £3000. The growth in the number of residential establishments financed in this way was unprecedented. From 1979 to 1990 the number of places in private residential homes for older people increased from 37,000 to 98,000 and central government expenditure on paying for people living in them increased from £10 million to £1.2 billion (Oldman 1991, pp.4–5). The Audit Commission pointed out that this was a 'perverse incentive', operating against the policy of community care, in that resources which could otherwise have been used for care in the community were locked up in costly residential provision, through this social security-funded arrangement for payment (Audit Commission 1986). These dramatic developments led some writers to a particular view of the origins of the community care reforms:

> The reforms were not primarily driven by a desire to improve the relations between the various statutory authorities or to improve services for elderly people, or to help those emerging from mental hospital. They were driven by the need to stop the haemorrhage in the social security budget and to do so in a way that would minimise political outcry and not give additional resources to the local authorities themselves...these were hurried ideas pushed through to meet a crisis. (Lewis and Glennerster 1996, p.8)

Sir Roy Griffiths, a supermarket executive who was already an advisor on health and welfare to the Conservative government, initiated the process of reform which was designed to address the crisis. Griffiths' terms of reference required him to focus on the utilisation rather than the adequacy of resources. He was asked 'to review the way in which public funds are used to support community care policy and to advise the Secretary of State on the options for action which would improve the use of these funds as a contribution to more effective community care' (Griffiths Report 1988, p.1).

The White Paper, *Caring for People* (1989), and the legislation which followed the Griffiths Report (1988) demonstrated the government's determination to cease the open-ended commitment to funding residential care from the social security budget and promoted as an alternative a mixed market of community care in which local authority social services departments[1] would be enablers rather than providers, co-ordinating and purchasing care rather than providing services directly. Six objectives were identified for the proposed system (Department of Health 1989):

- to promote the development of domiciliary, day and respite care to enable people to live in their own homes

- to provide support for carers

- to make proper assessment of need and case management the cornerstone of high quality care

- to promote a flourishing independent sector

- to clarify the responsibilities of agencies, particularly with respect to the NHS and local authorities

- to secure better value for taxpayers' money.

Within this system, the National Health Service and Community Care Act (1990) gave a gatekeeping role to social services departments in specifying that it was for local authorities to decide which needs to meet and how to meet them. To provide the resources to meet those needs, central government transferred the care element for places in residential establishments from the social security budget to social services departments in the form of a special transitional grant. (This was not new funding and in addition many social services departments found themselves implementing the National Health Service and Community Care Act (1990) in the context of wider local government budget cuts.)

The implementation of the National Health Service and Community Care Act (1990) changed fundamentally the operation of social services departments and the practice of social work. The Act ended social services departments' dominant provider position. Social work continued but in a different form and in a different context shaped by three inter-related developments, which were to have significant implications for social workers and front-line managers: marketisation, managerialism and consumerism. Each of these developments is considered in turn.

Marketisation

Although not part of the Thatcher governments' earliest efforts to extend the impact of market forces, which concentrated on health, education, pensions and housing (Le Grand and Robinson 1984; Papadakis and Taylor-Gooby 1987), community care was eventually subjected to this common policy of market-oriented reform (Le Grand 1993). Accordingly, when funds were transferred from the social security system to local government for community care, the imperative to create a community care market, with competition between providers, was sustained by central government's insistence that 85 per cent of the financing had to be spent on the independent sector. Social services departments were expected to make clear how they proposed to stimulate market activity where independent providers were not currently available, and various ways in which social services departments could promote a community care market were outlined: by setting clear service specifications, stimulating the independent sector and floating off some of their own services (Department of Health 1989, paras. 3, 4, 6).

The radical changes in the basis on which community care was to be provided represented the introduction of 'quasi-markets' (Le Grand 1993). The state, through delegation to social services departments, became primarily a funder with services provided by a variety of suppliers operating in competition with each other. The method of funding also changed, with budgets allocated on the basis of assessments by social workers, increasingly redesignated as 'care managers'. These quasi-markets were to differ from 'pure' markets in a number of important respects. For example, there would be competition between service suppliers but, in contrast with 'pure' markets, suppliers would not necessarily be privately owned nor would they necessarily be required to make profits. On the demand side, consumer purchasing power would be not in cash but in a budget confined to the purchase of a specific service. The service user would not necessarily exercise the final choice concerning purchasing decisions. Such decisions would be made on the basis of the recommendations of the care manager[2] (Le Grand 1990).

The establishment of quasi-markets drew social workers and front-line managers into unfamiliar territory. Along with parallel service changes instituted by the Children Act (1989), the community care reforms signalled the break-up of the role of social services departments as the providers of generic social work services. This intensified tendencies towards greater professional specialisation. In addition, assessment was separated from direct service provision as clear demarcation lines were drawn between purchasers and providers and working relationships were formulated on the basis of explicit contracts and specifications. Accordingly, when services such as home care or respite residential care were needed, instead of turning automatically to in-house colleagues social workers and front-line managers had to consider what was on offer from a number of suppliers. Rather than making assessments and acting as advocates for the allocation of in-house resources on the basis of their assessments, they were drawn into juggling budgets between the competing needs of service users and allocating those budgets between different service suppliers. As they moved into this unfamiliar territory of quasi-markets, their organisational base was itself being simultaneously transformed.

Managerialism

The emphasis on community care markets brought very different responsibilities to social services departments. As a result, they not only had to define and refine their new role in the market but also had to work through a process of substantial change in their internal organisational structures and cultures. As elsewhere in the transformation of the welfare state, a key component in shifting social services into organisational alignment with market forces was managerialism (Clarke, Cochrane and McLaughlin 1994; Pollitt 1990). A generic model of management, which minimised the differences between private sector business management and the public sector (Farnham and Horton 1993; Pollitt 1990, p.27), was seen as having the potential to breathe new life into social services (Audit Commission 1988; Local Government Training Board 1985), thus equipping social services departments for the challenges of managing the community care market. As part of wider managerial changes in social services, management in community care was regarded as having a number of elements:

- strategic vision – a clear sense of direction usually embodied in a mission statement
- common values – ownership of values throughout the social services department which were consistent with the organisation's *raison d'être*
- customer care – including complaints procedures
- performance review – by inspectorates

- budgetary procedures – which reflected strategic priorities
- clear leadership – from senior managers.

These elements were to be located within the overarching framework of the three 'E's: economy, efficiency and effectiveness (Audit Commission 1983). Senior managers were exhorted to take the lead in establishing this framework through conceiving strategy, planning change, defining and measuring needs and establishing priorities and targets. In short, they were encouraged to see themselves as having a strategic role as they surveyed the 'market environment' and deployed resources in pursuit of value-for-money services, through a centralised management command structure which replicated the characteristics of the private sector (Hoggett 1991).

The significance of the new managerial structures and cultures was not confined to senior managers. The scope of the managerial changes in community care is indicated in this comment by Sir Roy Griffiths, originator of many of the changes which were implemented:

> The proposals involve significant changes in role for a number of professional and occupational groups. In many cases their implementation will more sharply focus developments which are already taking place within professions. For example, many social services staff already have a managerial function but my approach will give this added emphasis, for example in the development of skills needed to buy in services. Other new skills particularly in the design of successful management accounting systems and the effective use of the information produced by them, will be needed. The changing role of Social Services authorities might also allow them to make more productive use of the management abilities and experience of all their staff including those who are not fully qualified social workers. (Griffiths Report 1988, p.25)

As this quotation illustrates, the cultivation of management abilities among social workers was a key aspect of the reforms. The new structures and cultures were intended to penetrate the day-to-day practice of social work and to change the nature of that practice. As a result, there was a substantial move away from approaches to social work which were therapeutic or which stressed the importance of social casework. Instead social workers were required to act as care *managers*, putting together *packages* of care for individuals, on the basis of their assessments of need and the identification of services to meet those needs from the quasi-*market*. Indicative of this shift in the nature of social work was the production, by the Central Council for Education and Training in Social Work, of training materials for social workers on topics such as purchasing and contracting (CCETSW 1992, 1994). Social workers were expected to have skills in assessing services required by individual service users, make judgements about how and by whom those services would be delivered and manage budgets in ways which ensured that value-for-money services were provided. Any specific skills traditionally associated with social work did not seem to be highly rated. The valued skills appeared to be managing budgets and using computerised recording and information systems (Harris 1998a; White 1999). It is important, however, not to depict these developments as an 'iron cage'. (For example, in Chapter Two, Morrison explores her team's approach to integrating inter-personal social work skills with a computerised assessment system.)

Consumerism

The introduction of markets into community care represented, at least rhetorically, a shift from a concern with providing services to the experience of receiving services (Barnes 1997, Chapter 2); a change in focus from service provider to service user or, as some preferred, consumer or customer. This new emphasis on the service user's preferences was reinforced in government guidance on how the community care system was to develop following the implementation of the reforms: 'The individual service user and normally, with his or her agreement, any carers should be involved throughout the assessment and care management process. They should feel that the process is aimed at meeting their wishes' (Department of Health 1990a, p.25). Involvement of service users and carers was thus seen as integral to assessment and care management and any failure to pursue their involvement, in accordance with the provisions of natural justice, could render a local authority liable to judicial review (Payne 1995, p.104). In addition, the establishment of complaints procedures offered the opportunity for redress (Department of Health 1990a), based on models from the commercial world.

This brand of public sector consumerism was pushed forward by Major's Citizen's Charter (Prime Minister 1991). The stated purpose of the Charter was to improve the quality of public services and to make them responsive to their users (Prime Minister 1991, p. 2): 'through these charters the citizen can increasingly put pressure upon those responsible for providing services to deliver them to a high standard rather as commercial competition puts consumer pressure on to the performance of private sector organisations' (Prime Minister 1991, p.1). The Citizen's Charter had four main themes:

- to improve the quality of public services
- to provide choice between competing providers

- to tell citizens what service standards are and how to act when service is unacceptable
- to give full value for money within a tax bill the nation can afford.

The publication of the Citizen's Charter was the prelude to the publication of a number of specific charters. The Conservative government produced a framework for and guidance on the production of Community Care Charters (Department of Health 1994a) as part of the Charter initiative. The emphasis was on simple output measures through which performance could be measured in individual services, against indicators drawn up by the Audit Commission. The implicit model was one of individual customers consuming services which had been inefficient thus far and which needed to be made more efficient by being made accountable to them.

The porduction of Community Care Charters represented official recognition of the importance of consumerism. From the early 1990s onwards, the range of language used in debates about community care narrowed across the political spectrum. The Conservative government, as we have seen, presented a strategy of empowering the individual citizen as a consumer (or customer) of community care; a strategy to be achieved by transferring services outside the public sector and setting in place quasi-market arrangements. In parallel, the Labour Party articulated a new emphasis on consumerism as a means of empowering individuals against what was depicted as a previously bureaucratic and domineering welfare state (Taylor-Gooby 1987, pp.199–201) with calls for the reallocation of power from the state to the individual (Pierson 1991, pp.196–7). The emergence of a political consensus around consumerism was evident on a number of key points (Labour Party 1991; Prime Minister 1991):

- Services need to be flexible in meeting individual needs.
- Individuals should have more say in how their needs are met.
- Services should be specified and standards set for them.
- Service users should have access to complaints procedures.

From this point onwards, consumerism occupied an ambiguous position in community care in a way which opens it up to different definitions and dimensions than those intended originally (Clarke and Newman 1997). As we have seen, consumerism was first driven politically by the Conservative government, but in the implementation of the community care reforms, consumerism connected with wider movements for change and with a range of concerns about the experience of service users, from a variety of perspectives (see, for example, Beresford et al. 1997). The political consensus which coalesced around the consumerism of the community care reforms has been used to promote different political values and strategies (Hoggett 1991, p.243). For example, it has been argued that the language of participation, partnership and choice can be used to empower users of services (Biehal, Fisher and Sainsbury 1992; Smale and Tuson 1993). Thus, the stress on the involvement of service users unleashed forces counterproductive to the original intention of the Conservative government's reforms, stimulating demand and exposing needs in ways which politicised some service users (Baldock 1993, p.28). Service user movements have made three general claims (Pakulski 1997, p.80):

- The right to presence and visibility versus marginalisation.
- The right to dignifying representation versus stigmatisation.
- The right to identity and maintenance of lifestyle versus assimilation.

Out of this maelstrom of meanings and expectations surrounding consumerism, three themes have emerged which provide indicators for workers of how its potential might be developed (Clarke and Newman 1997, p.111):

- Services need to be responsive to social diversity.
- Attention needs to focus on service delivery and direct interaction with service users.
- An active view needs to be taken of service users, who should be regarded not as passive recipients but as participants in defining their needs.

Having reviewed the period in which the community care reforms took place, and identified the implications of three inter-related developments (marketisation, managerialism and consumerism) for social workers and front-line managers, the injunctions which emerged can be summarised as follows:

- Get to grips with the market.
- Spend money wisely in purchasing and rationing services.
- Learn the disciplines associated with managerialism.
- Put everything on the computer.
- Be attentive to the needs of individual service users.
- See service users as consumers/customers.

Enter the third way

The election of New Labour in 1997 heralded the introduction of the 'Third Way'. The Third Way contains elements of continuity with the previous Conservative governments' emphasis on increased productivity in the public sector and better value for money (Cabinet Office 1999, Chapter 2). It encompasses the commercial discipline of the Conservative governments and rejects the 'old ways of doing things', associated with social services departments in the pre-Thatcher era. The Third Way approach to community care is an aspect of the modernisation agenda for social services which continues to stress the importance of a consumer-focused strategy. It includes the following principles (Department of Health 1998a):

- Care should be provided to people in a way that supports their independence and respects their dignity.
- Services should meet people's specific needs.
- People should have a say in the services they get and how they are delivered.
- People should be able to have confidence in their local social services, knowing that they work to clear and acceptable standards, and that if those standards are not met, action can be taken to improve this.

These elements of continuity, from the previous Conservative governments through to New Labour's Third Way, were complemented by a new emphasis on improving the relationship between health and social services. This stemmed from the recognition that service users experience their needs in terms of the quality of their daily lives, rather than in the compartments and categories manufactured by health and social services. Accordingly, New Labour considers that success in individualising services depends on an integrated approach to service delivery. If service users' needs do not fit easily and neatly into organisational categories, changes need to be made to inter-professional structures, systems and working relationships in social and health care. This is seen as being cost-effective as well as providing increased accessibility for service users.

A raft of proposals has resulted from this element in Third Way thinking. For example, *Partnership in Action* stressed the need for joint commissioning, joint investment plans, improved co-ordination between the National Health Service and local authorities and pooling budgets (Department of Health 1998b). *Saving Lives: Our Healthier Nation* stressed that New Labour's goals would only be achieved by joint effort through more effective partnerships at the community level between the NHS, local authorities and other agencies (Department of Health 1999a). The Health Act (1999) offered the option of pooled budgets for service user groups and the Health and Social Care Act (2001) is set to establish Care Trusts, as health service bodies, capable of providing all health and social services for community care purposes.

This emphasis on closer integration of health and social services raises 'the prospect of services being defined and delivered in the interstices between organisations rather than within the existing structural forms... Both strategies for, and the practice of, community care are likely to move increasingly into the spaces between organisations' (Clarke 1996, pp.54–55). The problems and possibilities of such inter-professional developments are considered in the contributions from Roy and Watts (Chapter Four), Walters (Chapter Five) and Millen and Wallman-Durrant (Chapter Nine). These contributions encompass some of the organisational, planning and strategic dimensions involved in crossing professional boundaries, as well as some of the day-to-day practice issues emerging from the delivery of services which cross traditional demarcation lines. In doing so, they raise questions, which will continue to be explored. Does the closer integration of health and social services mean that these services, and the people who work in them, need to become similar as roles blur into each other? Or should they retain their distinctiveness in more precisely defined divisions of labour (Smale, Tuson and Statham 2000, p.187), while being more open to how they might influence each other's development? In the context of these questions, Millen and Wallman-Durrant (Chapter Nine) consider inter-professional rivalry, different approaches to service provision (see also Dalrymple and Burke 1995, p.72), pressures, constraints, objectives and expectations (see also Thompson 2000, p.137) – all of which illustrate some of the complexity to be faced by workers on the ground in delivering the Third Way's integrationist agenda.

What about the workers?

We have been outlining the wholesale transformation of community care which has occurred over the last ten years. In the process of doing so, it has become clear that developments such as marketisation, managerialism and consumerism have had significant implications for social workers and front-line managers and for the nature of social work. These implications point to a shift in the status and role of those workers, to which we now turn.

In the pre-Thatcher period, in social services, as elsewhere in the welfare state, professionals played an important role. Unlike the rule-bound operation of the social security system, in social services workers were involved in defining the needs of service users on an individual basis and allocating the resources to meet those needs. In other words, they were seen as the key to the implementation of social services policy through the exercise of professional discretion (Harris 1998b; Laffin and Young 1990), on the assumption that discretion would be exercised in the interests of service users.

The privileged position accorded to workers in social services changed with the coming to power of the Thatcher governments. A new set of assumptions shaped the approach adopted towards them. They were now portrayed as essentially self-interested, primarily concerned with furthering their position by increasing their sphere of influence and seeking to increase the budgets over which they had control. This set of assumptions became dominant in the argument made for markets in community care. Workers were defined as part of the problem (Harris and McDonald 2000). Only the introduction of markets, the government argued, would force them to change.

As part of the process of enforcing change through the introduction of quasi-markets in community care, there was a sea-change in the Conservative government's approach. Policy implementation was not to be left to the good intentions of well-meaning professionals, as was previously the case. Central government intervened directly by providing large quantities of 'guidance' – of an authoritative character and primarily drawn from official sources – the production of which was dominated by government employees (Payne 1996). This guidance was a key instrument in implementing policy, through the provision of detailed prescriptions for professional decision-making and practice.

Simultaneously, workers were experiencing an onslaught from managerialism, particularly as resource questions began to loom large in the mid-1990s, a year or two into the implementation of the reforms. Workers were soon managing the tension between needs and available resources. Were they meant to be identifying need and encouraging service user choice (being responsive to the consumerist agenda) or were they primarily to be concerned with rationing through standardised procedures (being responsive to the managerialist cost containment agenda)? Were they gatekeeping or setting up hurdles? As the reforms bedded down, some of these tensions were managed by the use of eligibility criteria and charging policies, with increased targeting in terms of dependency and risk. There has been surprisingly little interest in what happens to potential service users who are filtered out by eligibility criteria. This issue is explored by Fleming and McSparran in the second half of their contribution on empowerment as a participative process (Chapter Six) and by Tanner (Chapter Seven) in relation to prevention.

The impact of targeting on workers was profound. They were squeezed in the vice of exhortations to empower service users and their own increasing sense of disempowerment as a consequence of managerialism. This squeeze between representing the needs and aspirations of service users and representing the employing agency's cost containment policies is a recurring theme in the literature. For example:

> Within community care there is the potential conflict between the customer asserting her entitlement, by right as a citizen, to a particular service, and the care manager acting as the custodian of scarce public resources. (Langan and Clarke 1994, p.86)

> The care manager may be working on behalf of the user, but he or she is also working for an agency. The rights and needs of the individual user will often conflict with agency policies for distributing available resources between users; and needs that cannot be met may not be taken into account. (Banks 1995, p.110)

> The person making a community care assessment finds herself looking at least two ways. On the one hand she has heard the exhortation that service provision should be needs led and that services should fit the person, rather than the person be fit to the services; but she also knows that she is in the front line in the apparently permanent campaign of resource rationing. She is to contribute to user empowerment by enabling users to participate but she is also to be aware of her responsibilities as a gatekeeper to public resources. (Barnes 1997, p.95)

> …the difficulties [which are] created for the 'care manager' by the contradictory demands imposed on her by the community care reforms. On the one hand, she is responsible for assessing the client's needs and for ensuring these needs are met. On the other hand, she is responsible for allocating resources for these needs – and for the needs of her other clients – within the constraints of the budget she has been allocated. She thus has to reconcile the tension between her responsibility to her client and her responsibility for rationing social services resources. (Langan 2000, p.157)

This tension was captured in government guidance issued at the time of the community care reforms in which need was defined as: '*The requirements of individuals* to enable them to achieve, maintain or restore an acceptable level of social independence or quality of life, *as defined by the particular care agency or authority*' (Social Services Inspectorate 1991a, p.14, our emphasis).

It could be argued that this tension has existed since the establishment of social services departments. However, prior to the community care reforms, the impact on the worker of the form the tension took was very different. In relation to assessment for example, the worker acted as what might be termed an 'assessor-advocate' with the outcome of an assessment being used by the worker to advocate on the service user's behalf for services which were rationed elsewhere in the organisation. In other words, there was a separation of managerial and professional principles and of the spheres of influence in which they came into play. One of the effects of the reforms was to integrate professional and managerial principles and, as a consequence:

> to reshape the nature and conditions of discretion within social work. In the old...regime, discretion was a complex process in which professional judgement could be exercised within statutory and bureaucratic framings ... [Now] the devolution of managerial responsibilities (particularly in relation to resources and budgets) is intended both to 'empower the front line' of organisations and to constrain professional autonomy by having professionals internalise budgetary disciplines. The result is that professional processes and categories of evaluation are compounded with managerial categories of cost, efficiency and risk. Such 'hybrid' calculations intensify pressures on those performing such roles... (Clarke 1996, pp.58–59)

This could sound like a counsel of despair for workers, weighed down by the inherent tensions in the community care system, which were built into its fabric from the time of the reforms. In the rest of the book, it becomes clear that there are workers who, with the support of their employing social services department, have not just reacted with passive acceptance to these developments. Instead, they are confronting the tensions and actively engaging with the changes which have taken and are taking place, as well as initiating changes themselves. Where did they find this progressive potential in community care?

Partnership and participation

As we have seen, the critique of professionals, which underpinned the community care reforms, led to a strong emphasis on the involvement of service users in assessment of their needs and decisions about services to meet them. This emphasis ran through the White Paper, *Caring for People* (1989), and the subsequent government guidance on community care, mentioned in the previous section. By the mid-1990s it had moved from being the 'new idea' which progressive authorities were adopting in order to renew and revitalise their relationships with those using their services, to a legislative requirement…and a job description for officials within both health and social care agencies. If the claims of statutory agencies were to be believed, virtually everyone was doing it, although on close inspection just what people were doing and the degree of change it represented showed considerable variation. (Barnes 1997, p.89)

Despite its emergence from a critique of professionalism, this promotion of partnership with service users resonated with existing attempts by some workers to shift the nature of their practice in the direction of working as much as possible alongside service users, rather than for them, and, at least rhetorically, the official concern with partnership embraced some of the concerns of service user groups. For other workers, partnership struck at the heart of their professional identity (Biggs 1997) because they regarded their expertise as lying in the delineation of service users' problems (Marsh and Fisher 1992).

Unfortunately, when it came to the implementation of the community care reforms, the progressive potential of partnership was all too easily over-shadowed by preoccupation with such matters as the purchaser–provider split, the quasi-market, the design of assessment forms and the fine-tuning of eligibility criteria, rather than the practical and philosophical challenges involved in moving towards partnership with service users:

> Involvement in assessment and developing strategies for working on problems is not just a question of responding to a series of pre-defined questions on the assessment schedule. It involves negotiations; the ability to work with effective problem solving strategies which have been developed by the people already involved; the ability to recognise when those strategies have themselves become a problem and how that can be addressed. It involves drawing on the insights which service users and their carers have developed into their needs, individually and jointly, and then working out how they can be enabled to meet them, again both individually and jointly. Fundamentally it involves recognising that assessment is not just a question of applying professional knowledge, but also of learning from the knowledge of those they are assessing… If carers and users are to experience the…procedures as empowering at the individual level, then as much attention must be given to the development of partnership skills among those working at the front line as was given to the development of criteria, procedures and structures for the implementation of assessment and care management. (Barnes 1997, p.140)

The lack of attention to the challenges posed by partnership, once it became 'official', led some authors to suggest that the word is 'used to describe anything from token consultation to a total devolution of power and control' (Braye and Preston-Shoot 1995, p.102). Its variable and uneven use is represented in the allegation that it has become a 'buzz-word' (Thompson 2000, p.135). Despite fluid use of the term, it has a core element: 'Partnership can mean anything from the most cautious interpretations to the most radical... What links both ends of the spectrum is the notion that *service users should be included as far as possible as fellow citizens* in the decision-making processes which affect their lives' (Dalrymple and Burke 1995, p.64, our emphasis). This potential of partnership to point beyond consumerism as an identity to citizenship as a status is an important shift and underpins the contributions to this book. The contributors are approaching the people with whom they work as consumer-citizens (White and Harris 1999), rather than seeing them simply as customers in the community care marketplace.

Such movements towards partnership are not achieved by a 'faceless representative of the organisation but by a genuine human being, a fellow citizen willing to share in tackling a problem with others' (Smale, Tuson and Statham 2000, p.209). This sentiment has an appeal across a range of social work perspectives. For example, 'constructive social work', which is influenced by postmodernism, sees partnership and participation as central (Parton and O'Byrne 2000, p.187) in ensuring that the views and interests of service users are prioritised:

> In the constructive approach professionals bring their own knowledge to the helping situation but that knowledge is not accorded more authority than the person's own knowledge. Rather the social worker's investment in process is to assist people in identifying resources and opportunities which may have been hidden from them or framed in ways which were not helpful. In this view, a social work relationship is a partnership, with each partner bringing something of value to the conversations. (Parton and O'Byrne 2000, p.184)

If partnership is regarded as a process, with a range of practices existing along a continuum, it will come 'in all shapes and sizes' (Marsh 1998, p.199). On this continuum, partnership surfaces the possibility of competing views and perceptions about needs and the question of how these are to be negotiated in a participative manner: 'A process known as principled negotiation...applies particularly where perspectives may differ. It focuses on interests which can be heard and deemed legitimate rather than positions that give rise to a battle of wills, and seeks to identify options which best meet the declared interests of all parties' (Braye and Preston-Shoot 1995, p.118).

More fundamentally, partnership also raises the question of power differences between the service user and the worker (Ellis 1993). There is a need to consider the balance of power and how power can be shared:

> For users to be fully involved practitioners have to recognise and acknowledge the power differences that exist and seek to minimise those differences. Minimising differences requires us to develop strategies that are based on support from managers and colleagues and understanding from service users. For strategies to be successful there needs to be recognition of the *opposing* and *supporting* factors which impinge on the process of involving users. For example, one of the *opposing forces* is the unequal power relationships and differing values perspectives that exist between professionals and their colleagues and professionals and service users. *Supporting forces* include the commitment to user involvement and the relinquishing of power. (Dalrymple and Burke 1995, p.144, emphasis original)

This is an important issue. The term 'partnership' should not be used simplistically in order to imply that participants have equal power, as Barry's discussion of Guardianship (Chapter Eight) demonstrates. She considers an area of practice which has often been regarded as having coercive connotations but shows that even in such an area there are gains to be made from recognition of the power distribution between worker and service user and open discussion about how power is used. In some areas of practice it is possible to go further and attempt, through a commitment to partnership, to redistribute power between the parties. This is a crucial aspect of the approach to individual assessments advocated by Morrison (Chapter Two), which involves service user participation in the construction of written information about them:

> Knowledge of recorded information is the means by which users can verify what is written about them and their situations and correct inaccurate information. It gives back control to users... Sharing information in an open and honest way demonstrates respect (Dalrymple and Burke 1995, p.140)

Redistribution of power is also a characteristic of the strategic approaches to service planning and development described by Lalani and Whiting (Chapter Three) and Walters (Chapter Five). Developing partnership in service planning has been more common than consultation with individual service users about their day-to-day experience (Barnes 1997, p.85). The latter is considered by Fleming and McSparran (Chapter Six) and Tanner (Chapter Seven).

These examples, which are explored in depth in the relevant chapters, suggest the need to recognise power relationships overtly, by asking the following questions (Braye and Preston-Shoot 1995, p.119):

- What level of partnership is envisaged?
- What is negotiable within the power relationship and what is not?
- What are the limits to choice?
- What are the rights and responsibilities of each party?

The use of these questions encourages reflection and addresses potential conflicts openly. Lack of openness and exchange in the interests of superficial consensus with service users undermines partnership. Ellis found that service user cynicism about partnership stemmed from workers withholding information, not making criteria clear, using professional language and failing to check things out (Ellis 1993).

All of this suggests that the nature of partnership is susceptible to change according to circumstances (see Chapters Two, Three, Five and Six). As the relationships between partners change with circumstances, the worker needs to be able to analyse the nature of the partnership relationships (Smale, Tuson and Statham 2000, pp.186–7). The reflective stance towards partnership adopted by the contributors to this book stands in stark contrast to that of workers who say 'we do all that already' (Marsh and Fisher 1992). The former's stance takes partnership with service users seriously and seeks to foster it by building trust, the glue which holds partnership together. Trust can be thought of as having six components (Barnes and Prior 1996):

- *acceptance* of the validity of the other's experiences, knowledge and interpretations
- *confidence* that the other has the capacity to make appropriate judgements about how to act in varying circumstances
- *respect* for the role of the other as an active contributor to the relationship
- *honesty* towards the other in a willingness to share all relevant information about the relationship
- *reciprocity of duty*, recognising that each partner in the relationship has responsibilities towards the other
- *reciprocity of interest*, recognising that each partner has their own goals which they will want to pursue through the relationship.

A key aspect of community care services which has often failed to inspire such trust has been the reaction to the needs of minority ethnic groups and communities. There has been a legacy of limited responsiveness and inappropriate service provision, which was well documented around the time of the implementation of the community care reforms (Atkin and Rollings 1993; Butt 1994; Walker and Ahmad 1994) and which illustrated the need to extend the concept of partnership to the development of services for minority ethnic groups (Dalrymple and Burke 1995, p.65).

At the time of the community care reforms there was some scepticism about how they would play out with regard to minority ethnic groups because the impact of racial disadvantage was sidelined in them (National Institute for Social Work 1990; Patel 1990). Following the reforms, some authors argued that minority ethnic groups could stand to gain from the potential for greater flexibility in service arrangements and the trend towards more systematic assessment of the needs of individual service users (Ahmad and Atkin 1996, p.4; Blakemore and Boneham 1994, p.134; Walker and Ahmad 1994). Such authors acknowledge that while this is not the same as dealing with the fundamental disadvantage faced by minority ethnic groups, there are possibilities for change in the community care field and that this is preferable to continuing simply to describe the problems. Such an approach is exemplified by Lalani and Whiting in Chapter Three, which provides an honest and thoughtful account of seeking to engage in partnership with minority ethnic communities in the locality in which they were working. Their account not only raises issues about how existing services can be adapted in ways which make them more appropriate to the needs of a wider constituency (Atkin 1991), but also considers the development of services through organisations which the minority ethnic groups themselves identified as their preferred options and the establishment of forms of service provision which were managed by their own communities. As such, their chapter could be used to generate a range of questions about whether the ways in which social services work with other groups and communities require similar realignment (Payne 1995, p.183). Perhaps the mode of working which they describe could be extended as a more routine aspect of partnership practice, particularly given the emphasis on prevention as part of the modernisation programme for social care (Wistow *et al.* 2001).

Concluding comment

The gale of change in community care shows no sign of having blown itself out; change looks set to remain on the agenda. The contributors to the book indicate in the following chapters some of the ways in which that agenda might be tackled. Drawing on lessons from their past experience, they provide glimpses of how practice might develop in the future. These glimpses are brought together in Hallett's final chapter in which he explores the prospects and possibilities for good practice. In different ways, each of the chapters identifies the potential contribution social work can continue to make to community care. In whatever configuration of services and settings social work is located in years to come, the contributors provide grounds for optimism that a commitment to partnership and participation will prove crucial in sustaining good practice.

Notes

1   The term 'social services departments' is used throughout, as the book is based on contributions from an English social services department.

2   Except for those service users purchasing services for themselves following the arrangements set in place under the Direct Payments Act (1996).

Chapter Two

Improving the Quality
of Written Assessments
A Participative Approach

Ann Morrison

Introduction

Assessment is a central aspect of social work practice. The *Care Management and Assessment: Practitioners' Guide*, for example, states that care management and assessment lie at the heart of community care. The Guide recognises that needs are unique to the individual concerned and that they should be identified and addressed in a systematic way (Social Services Inspectorate 1991a, p.115). The implication is that without the use of assessment, social workers would simply respond to events and intervene in people's lives in an unplanned way, instead of being people 'who can organise, systematise and rationalise the knowledge gathered, with a gift for sensitivity in taking into account the uniqueness of each person's situation' (Coulshed and Orme 1998, p.21). However, despite widespread acknowledgement of the centrality of assessment, it has often been regarded as self-evident and unproblematic (Milner and O'Byrne 1998, p.7). This is particularly the case with the topic of this chapter, namely written assessments. They are often seen as simply the drudgery which has to be undertaken after the inter-personal work, seen as the real business of assessment, has taken place. In contrast to the relative neglect of the written assessment, the chapter stresses the crucial importance of the quality of the writing and provides a framework for thinking about how that quality can be developed.

The introduction of the National Health Service and Community Care Act (1990) is often blamed for a major change in assessment practice. While the legislation provided 'much needed definitions of assessment' it also 'had the effect of leaving social workers in a vacuum between the old and new styles of working and/or encouraging a checklist mentality' (Milner and

O'Byrne 1998, p.19). Warwickshire Social Services Department decided, at the outset of implementing the community care reforms, to discourage a checklist mentality by not having a tick-box format. Instead, a free-writing approach was adopted, within a structure of core elements which were to be covered by assessments. These elements are:

- biographical details
- self-perceived needs and wishes
- self-care
- health
- informal network
- support and service network.

Despite this freer format, the Adult Team[1], in which the work described below took place, was motivated to examine its approach to assessment as a result of team members' dissatisfaction with the end product (the written assessment) given to service users. The quality of assessments which were likely to produce a major change in someone's circumstances was seen as particularly significant in terms of the consequences for service users' lives. A wider departmental analysis of the quality of assessment reports also showed that many reports were flawed in relation to style, sensitivity, grammar and accuracy. The analysis was commissioned by the Director to examine all written reports presented to five Resource Allocation Panels throughout the county, and was conducted by an experienced social worker and a nursing manager from the health authority. In addition to the deficits noted, the report highlighted wide variation in practice and indicated that this was an area of training that needed development. Despite the evidence of flawed reports, managers found it difficult and time-consuming to correct written work and queried whether it was their role to do so. This was in contrast to reports emanating from practitioners in child care teams, where work was scrutinised before presentation to service users, managers and outside agencies.

The team's attitude to the quality of its assessments echoed some of the concerns expressed in the literature referenced in this chapter that good practice stems from open-minded and comprehensive assessments which avoid a narrow service-oriented focus (see, for example, Coulshed and Orme 1998, p.25). Such good practice in assessment paints a picture of an individual person, clarifying the person's self-perceived views and wishes and acknowledging the centrality of the service user's voice (Coulshed and Orme 1998; Dalrymple and Burke 1995; Thompson 2000). This involvement of the service user in the process is built around self-assessment in which 'the real feelings, needs and wishes of the individual can be discovered' (Hepinstall 1992, quoted in Dalrymple and Burke 1995, p.115). If the process incorporates the views of those being assessed, professional assumptions about need may well be challenged (Morris 1993).

In line with just such concerns, the team wanted to improve assessment reports in ways which reflected the values of social work and the principles of practice in the community care field. In order to distinguish their practice from that of health professionals, social work practitioners often quote the 'values of social work'. In order to be explicit about its values base, the team used CCETSW's 'Value Requirements' (CCETSW 1998, p.7):

- to identify and question our own values and prejudices, and their implications for practice

- to respect and value uniqueness and diversity, and recognise and build on strengths

- to promote people's rights to choice, privacy, confidentiality and protection, while recognising and addressing the complexities of competing rights and demands

- to assist people to increase their control over and improve the quality of their lives .

- to identify, analyse and take action to counter discrimination, racism, disadvantage, inequality and injustice, using strategies appropriate to role and context

- to practise in a manner that does not stigmatise or disadvantage either individuals, groups or communities.

In accordance with these values, the team wanted to emphasise that the written product should embody respect for the individuals being assessed and should be written in a format that was comprehensible and meaningful to them. The team worked on a number of issues: the format of and audiences for the assessment report; learning to write better assessments; how assessments can be improved; and the end product. These issues are now considered through a narrative of the stages the team has been through in seeking to improve the quality of its written assessments. These, or similar stages, could be used by other teams wishing to work on this aspect of their practice.

Stage one: asking basic questions

At a regular monthly practice meeting, we decided to share our written assessments. At the first session practitioners were asked to contribute a list of questions, so that we could plan how we would tackle the issue of improvement. The first session produced the following questions:

- What is a good assessment?

- What is a good multi-disciplinary assessment?

- Who is the assessment for?

- How should the assessment reflect departmental procedures?

- How are the values of social work and community care reflected in the assessment process?

- How is it written? (Is it easily understood? Does it contain social work jargon?)

- What was the response from the service user to her/his assessment?

The questions posed by individual practitioners provided the framework for our agenda to improve written assessments. The questions provoked a good deal of discussion, as practitioners reflected on their own assumptions about written assessments. This process reinforced the importance of 'tailoring interventions to specific situations' rather than looking for 'off-the-peg solutions' (Thompson 2000, p.143).

Stage two: auto-critique

At the second session we agreed that everyone would bring a copy of an assessment that s/he had written. The assessments would be shared in confidence with the rest of the team, highlighting any aspects of the assessment process that the worker had found particularly difficult. The team would read each assessment from a service user's viewpoint and offer constructive criticism to individual practitioners. The exercise worked extremely well, as team members highlighted words and terms with which they were unhappy in their own and other workers' reports, and commended others. During this exercise, we identified two main areas of difficulty: first, the use of social work jargon or technical terms; second, our inclination to write negatively about service users' difficulties, which we viewed as contradictory to the social work values of respect and dignity of the individual user, of assisting people to have increased control over their lives and of practising in a manner which does not stigmatise or disadvantage. Two members of the team volunteered to collate examples of how users' needs could be expressed more positively in assessments. Some of the examples were as given in Table 2.1:

Table 2.1	
Negative phrases	**Positive phrases**
Mrs Brown is incontinent.	Mrs Brown cannot always manage her continence/has accidents when using the toilet/manages with the use of pads.
Mr Green is immobile.	Mr Green can walk with the use of aids/needs help to walk or to get on the bed/chair/toilet.
Ms Purple has dementia.	Ms Purple is forgetful/worried that she is losing her memory/has periods of confusion.
Mrs White cannot express her views.	Mrs White finds it difficult to respond to direct questions but has indicated what is important to her.

This exercise was more difficult than it appeared. We found that we often replaced one negative term by another piece of jargon. Our first improvement to 'immobile' stated that Mr Green needed assistance with mobilisation and transfers – less negative, but just as incomprehensible. Our realisation that we needed to question statements more than once was a step on the road to becoming more user-centred in our writing.

Further sessions were planned by the team to examine our assessment procedures. These included: how to incorporate reports from other professionals and agencies; how to portray the different views of users and carers without overemphasising conflict or breaking confidences; how to minimise intervention in service users' lives; and how to gather information. These elements are touched on throughout the rest of the chapter.

Stage three: identifying skills

The team began the process of identifying the skills that practitioners needed to undertake an assessment. In doing so, it was recognised that assessments are multi-purpose documents: a source of management information, a tool in deciding the allocation of scarce resources and an exercise undertaken with and for the service user.

The *Care Management and Assessment: Managers' Guide* (Social Services Inspectorate 1991b, p.114) suggests the following prerequisites for assessing needs:

- inter-personal skills in establishing partnerships with users and carers
- facility for open communication and active learning
- understanding of Black and ethnic minority needs
- ability to synthesise the assessments of different agencies into a coherent whole
- capacity for defining desired outcomes with users and carers
- skill in working with interpreters and facilitators
- capacity to interpret eligibility criteria.

Smale and Tuson (1993) elaborate on the skills upon which assessment rests:

- skills of marginality (the capacity to join with people but remain impartial)
- skills in challenging (confronting people with behaviours obstructing need resolution)
- skills in conceptualisation (the ability to pattern and make sense of data in whichever form it is presented)
- skills in reframing (the ability to help redefine circumstances in ways which lead to problem resolution).

Other skills are identified by Seed and Kaye (1994):

- sustaining motivation
- gathering and recording data
- observation, reflection and planning
- self-insight to make objective judgements on another's needs
- recording in ways that makes sense to the reader, who does not necessarily know anything about the client
- the ability to use a computer.

A good assessment is one that incorporates and reflects all these skills. How the team attempted to take account of them is the focus of the next section.

Stage four: incorporating principles

The Department of Health Guides list the benefits of care management, emphasising the importance of a needs-led approach, the commitment to individual care planning, and specifying desired outcomes. They state that there has been an emergence of a growing consensus on the values that underpin community care. The *Practitioners' Guide* states that 'it will be a fundamental requirement...that all participants understand and own the values and objectives which underpin the move from a service-led to a needs-led approach' (Social Services Inspectorate 1991a, p.5). The values are presented in terms of recognising rights – of citizenship, independence, privacy, dignity, individuality, individual choice – and promoting individuals' aspirations and abilities. In Warwickshire, we developed our own guidelines in preparation for implementing the National Health Service and Community Care Act (1990). These guidelines are known as the value principles of assessment and care management.

Having shared our written assessments with each other and raised our awareness of their strengths and shortcomings, the team then worked on how the principles of community care could be incorporated into our written assessments. This resulted in the following suggestions.

Empowerment

The *Managers' and Practitioners' Guides* state that users should be fully and actively involved in the assessment process. Carers should also be given the opportunity to contribute and advocates should be sought when a person finds it difficult to express their views. We interpreted this as requiring that the assessment should state how the individual was involved in writing up the assessment and how her/his views were gained.

Equality

The *Guides* describe the rights of citizenship as offering equal access to service provision, irrespective of gender, race, or disability. We agreed to interpret this as meaning that assessments should always consider the implications for service users of ethnic origin, age, gender, disability, sexual orientation, culture and beliefs. In practice this could mean translating assessments into other languages, into Braille or transcribing them on to tapes.

Privacy

The *Guides* use the helpful phrase 'intruding no more than is necessary to achieve the agreed purpose' (Social Services Inspectorate 1991a, 1991b, p.7). Our interpretation of this was that practitioners should seek permission before taking notes and make an agreement with the service user about whether to include all details in the assessment, paying particular attention to wishes concerning intimate or personal details. Team members reflected that it was not essential to include, for instance, lengthy life histories or intimate personal or sexual histories, unless the service user wished.

Respect

The *Guides* refer to the value of respect for the independence of individuals and their right to self-determination and to take risks, minimising any restraint upon that freedom of action. The team felt that this principle is the one that should guide us in producing a well-presented, clear and grammatical document. Service users' names should be given in full and the assessment should not appear too familiar or casual. An emphasis on the positive aspects of an individual's life and abilities, as opposed to writing what a person cannot do, demonstrates this respect. The assessment should be written in an open and honest manner.

Individuality

It is interesting to note that the *Guides* do not define individuality. We interpreted this to mean that workers should use their writing skills to paint a picture of the individual person. Service users and carers should be asked how they like to be described and whether they would like to write some sections or to describe their own history. This is particularly relevant when stating a person's views and wishes. Workers can record actual words used, for example, 'I've been a bit down recently', as opposed to 'Mrs X is depressed'. We agreed that medical terms should not be used unless the service user understands them. We felt that even if the service user understands the medical terms, they may still require supplementing with the service user's explanation of them. For example, 'Mrs X has been described by her doctor as having oedematous legs; she describes this as her legs feeling tight and painful'.

Partnership

The *Guides'* definition of partnership refers to making agency agreements and valuing the contributions of different agencies. In Warwickshire we also included service users and carers in the term 'partnership', to demonstrate our commitment to wide consultation. We agreed that full participation in decision-making could be shown by recording that the assessment had been shared with the user and carer and that they had signed it to indicate their agreement with its contents. Recording the contributors to the assessment shows partnership with other agencies.

Confidentiality

The *Guides* mention guaranteeing confidentiality, while acknowledging that the application of the values will not always be straightforward. We agreed to demonstrate this value in our written assessments, by emphasising that service users and carers must be able to have their views recorded separately and that these views should only be disclosed to the other party by agreement. In addition the service users' written permission should be obtained before consulting other professionals. There are dilemmas for practitioners in adhering to the principle of confidentiality. For example, a doctor may have diagnosed cancer, but have stated that the service user is unaware of the condition. The workers need to agree how this can be recorded. It may be that this needs discussion with the doctor and/or the carer to reach a consensus on what to record. The *Guides* indicate that one solution is to make the values explicit, and owned and shared by practitioners in all agencies in order to provide a solid foundation on which to build collaboration.

Consideration

Warwickshire defines consideration to mean 'a responsibility to provide services in a way that promotes the realisation of an individual's aspirations and abilities in all aspects of daily life. Service users can find the process of being assessed quite confusing. Workers need to explain the process carefully, giving as much written information as possible and trying to avoid duplication of other professionals' work' (Warwickshire Social Services Department 1996, p.3). The team found it very helpful when we invited service users and carers to come to a session and describe how it felt to be assessed. One carer stated that she did not wish to be told what was politically correct. This was in response to a practitioner who had insisted on the service user being described as 'learning disabled' rather than 'mentally handicapped'. The carer was also described in the assessment as being 'overprotective'. The team felt that it was crucial to reflect on how they would feel on seeing a written assessment on themselves and to question whether they would like to be described in particular ways. Our session with carers reinforced our view that assessments should reflect service users' feelings and not practitioners' own personal judgements.

We have found that service users find it much more difficult to comment on their assessments than carers. This may reflect their vulnerability, anxiety, fear or lack of comprehension. If they are reluctant to comment, it is even more important that we demonstrate that we have sought their views. It is good practice for workers to ask the service user if they can take notes and to read back what they have written in order to check for accuracy. In addition, assessments should be sent to users and carers for proof reading, whenever possible.

Responsiveness

Since the Access to Personal Files Act (1987), service users have had access to their files. Access to records, and the welcome requirement that service users should be given copies of their assessments and care plans, places a relatively new expectation on social workers to write clearly, objectively and sensitively. Open access to files enhances participation, gives back some of the power to the service user and is a demonstration of respect. Our assessments should indicate how we have given information to service users about their rights to see all records and their rights to access the representation and complaints procedure. Warwickshire Social Services Department now asks service users, as a standard part of our reviewing process, if they were given copies of their care plan and assessment, if they know how to obtain copies of their records and whether they know how to make a complaint.

Stage five: consolidating practice

Once we had agreed what an assessment should contain, in terms of the application of the social work values and community care principles, we agreed that we would continue to hold regular good practice sessions four times a year, on the basis that it is only by sharing our work that we can learn to improve it. Team members have led on topics which have included giving information, recording assessments on people with dementia, planning the assessment, what should and should not be recorded and how to record reviews. We have also considered how assessments for different service user groups, such as people with learning disabilities and people from minority ethnic communities, could be improved. We have circulated good assessment reports and refined our lists of useful phrases and unhelpful ones. We recommend that teams do this exercise themselves, as they will find their own 'howlers' and improvements. One of our later ones looked like Table 2.2.

Table 2.2 Examples of clearer writing	
Do not use	*Try instead*
Assessment	Agree with you what the problems are and what you need
Allocated (worker)	Own individual worker
Criteria (unless unavoidable)	We have lots of requests, so we have to make priorities
Dementia (unless diagnosed)	• Beginning to lose his/her memory • Can be confused/disorientated • Forgetful • Sometimes has episodes of confusion, anxiety, forgetfulness
Does not wish to disclose	Mrs X does not wish her personal history to be recorded here. She will be happy to disclose details, as she feels appropriate.

Some other useful phrases are:

Shown a potential for…

Main interest (in the community)…

Is dealing with…

No longer his/her normal self…

Which involved a traumatic loss…

Would support efforts to…

Experiences times of confusion /agitation…

Situation is very fragile…

Aware he/she is unable to do as much as he/she used to…

Risks associated with household appliances…

Has difficulty (with continence management) and sometimes/always uses a pad…

Has some problems recalling appointments and time. [Name] will need reminding about this.

Wants the chance to

Especially wants to…

Would like to…

A person who enjoys…

Led an active and varied life…

Happier with…

Worried he/she is beginning to lose his/her memory…

Tells me that…

The risks he/she faces are those to do with…

Increasing social isolation he/she faces…

Unable to express verbally how he/she feels…

Trusts the family/friend to make decisions on their behalf…

In relation to our conduct of assessments, it was agreed that a key element is planning and explaining the assessment process. We suggest that this starts on the first visit by giving information and leaflets, explaining the social work role, asking the service user's consent to consult others, asking whom they wish to be consulted, and indicating how long the assessment process is likely to take. We also agreed that we would ask service users regularly how they felt about their assessments, with feedback at all stages of the process – during the initial and further assessments and while monitoring and reviewing packages of care. The team agreed that we would ask service users directly about their assessment, for example, 'Have I represented your views accurately?' Or, 'Are you happy with how I've described what's happened in your life up to now?' Workers need to use an empowering approach, emphasising to service users that it is not difficult to change wording as this indicates that the assessment process has been a shared one. Where necessary workers should read out the assessment to service users or ask an interpreter to do so. Developing formats which make it easier for service users to understand their assessments is sometimes challenging. One team member has developed a format called 'Oi, it's my assessment!' This uses well-known symbols in work with people with learning disabilities.

In parallel with this work within the team, we established a dialogue with colleagues in the Information Strategy Team, which led to an improvement in the assessment printout from the computer system. The original ones had looked, to our mind offensively, like impersonal computer printouts with obtrusive lines, unnecessary dates and repetition of names. The revised version presents a clear narrative in a larger font.

While the service user is a key audience for the written assessment, multi-disciplinary panels and service providers also receive copies of assessments and their feedback is important. Health colleagues may comment on the quality of reports and this needs to be fed back to the writer. We found that some nurses who had contributed to assessments had never seen how their contributions had been included in the final product. We realised that we needed to pay attention to how we attributed professionals' views in our work and to offer the assessment to health professionals for their comments, with the service user's consent.

As far as service providers are concerned, one of our sessions was held with managers of residential and nursing homes and they were asked whether the assessments were accurate, helpful and stood the test of time. These professionals gave us some good tips. They suggested that often the sections on personal history were inaccurate or out of date or unnecessary. They suggested that their residents usually gave their own history and that other details could be added later. Dignity and privacy might be demonstrated in some instances by recording, for example, that 'Mr Yellow has had an eventful life and is willing to describe this himself to those for whom he considers it relevant'.

Other ways of improving assessments

In addition to the team's now established regular meetings to discuss and consolidate good practice (see Appendix One for an example) and invitations extended to a range of people outside the team to contribute their thoughts on the quality of our written assessments, two other strands were developed to improve assessments, not only in our team but also in other Adult Teams. The first was to develop a training package and the other was to write a guide on how to write an assessment.

Training sessions were provided for a large group of colleagues in Adult Teams. Three team members presented our work in order to demonstrate that improvements in social work practice can happen through reflection and discussion. We introduced a group of actors who played out a scenario of a social worker assessing a service user with her carer. We asked the audience to complete a section of an assessment, based on the scenario they had just witnessed. We then presented our material showing how assessments could be improved and asked participants to rewrite the first draft of their assessment. Everyone changed his or her first draft significantly. One practitioner changed hers from 'Ms Woods is immobile and cannot transfer' to 'Ms Woods is finding it increasingly difficult to walk and feels pains in her joints when rising or transferring from her chair'. Another practitioner changed 'Ms Woods is unable to self-medicate' to 'Ms Woods states that she sometimes forgets to take her tablets and would like to find a way to help her remember'. 'Ms Woods is demanding towards her son' became 'Ms Woods needs a lot of reassurance and contact from her son Malcolm'.

The changes the participants made in the second drafts of their assessments reflected a much more respectful and consultative approach to working with service users and carers. In their first drafts, some practitioners recorded things that had not been said or discussed during the play. They used phrases such as 'cognitive impairment', 'incontinence' and 'poor hygiene', which had not been spelled out or discussed with Ms Woods. One reported that the carer was stressed although he had not used that term. He had said he was worried. (The play was later video-taped so that it could be used at other training sessions.)

Feedback on the exercise of rewriting their assessments revealed that the participants saw it as a valued learning opportunity and for all of them it was the only occasion on which they had received any training on how to record and write assessments. They were keen to establish regular workshops in their own teams. The managers present acknowledged that they must demonstrate their commitment to improving quality by remembering to acknowledge good written work – improvements are not brought about simply by negative criticism.

Writing an assessment guide proved more difficult as we continually wanted to rewrite it as we learnt more. However, we have produced information that includes guidance on style, format and presentation. It emphasises the importance of discussing all written records with service users and informing them of their rights. We emphasise that the assessment process and the written assessment should reflect good social work practice and adherence to the values and principles outlined in this chapter. Some of the points in our guide at present are:

- An assessment should not include anything that cannot be substantiated. For example, medical diagnoses should not be included unless medical practitioners have confirmed them.

- Details of medication and dosages should not be included if there is any risk that they may be inaccurate.

- Service users should be consulted before intimate details are included, as they may not be relevant.

- The writer should confine him or herself to the areas of need and not write as if s/he is an advocate. Meeting needs is a separate stage of care management.

- The inclusion of other professionals' reports in the assessment can be tricky. We advise that it is crucial to name the source of information or to attach a separate report. It is important not to rewrite another professional's views as if they are your own.

- Two problematic areas are the diagnosis that has not been shared with the service user and a multi-disciplinary case conference which has made a decision that the social worker considers does not uphold the principles of service user involvement and empowerment. In both instances colleagues need to be challenged.

- We recommend that we adopt the same approach to colleagues from other disciplines that we recommend for ourselves, that is to give positive feedback to sensitive and objective contributions and ask for more factual details when needs are presented as recommendations.

Conclusions

We have not presented the work we have undertaken in a spirit of having all the answers. Writing good assessments is difficult, but they can be improved. In our experience, learning occurs through reflecting on our work collectively and engaging in exercises that make us think about what we have written. Notwithstanding the improvements which can be achieved by such an approach, we would not wish to minimise some of the dilemmas. These include:

- How to undertake good assessments quickly, especially if your manager is encouraging speed.

- Sometimes it appears impossible to highlight the positive aspects of a person's life and still obtain the required resource, which is linked to priority categories.

- It is not easy to present the conflicting views of carers and service users and still respect confidentiality.

We cannot offer solutions to all such dilemmas, but discussions with colleagues do help and, with practice, writing good assessments takes no longer than writing ones which are not so good.

A final set of questions, which we have found useful as reminders of how important this aspect of our work is, is as follows:

- Is this how I would want to be described?

- Is this how I would want my mother/father/partner/sister/brother assessed?

- Is the writing of good assessments a priority for me?

- Did I ask if I could take notes?

- Is this assessment needs-led or service-led?

- Have I remembered that the computer is only a tool?

- Does this assessment utilise inter-personal and other professional skills?

(An example of an assessment is provided in Appendix Two.)

Note

1   The team assesses adults, of whatever age, who have needs due to physical disabilities, learning disabilities or mental health problems. ('Age' does not appear in this connection in Warwickshire Social Services Department, because growing older is not regarded as a problem in itself.)

Chapter Three

Progressing Race Equality
Dynamics of Partnership

Mehrunnisa Lalani and Jon Whiting

Introduction

This chapter describes a process, which took place over several years, of developing community care services for the Black communities in a town in Warwickshire. It is a description of the difficulties we faced – and continue to face – and how we have sought to resolve them. The starting point for this process was an acknowledgement of the failure of the social services department to recognise and identify the needs of the Black communities and to provide services in a way that was sensitive to their needs. This was not an unusual situation. In the run-up to the National Health Service and Community Care Act (1990), it was claimed that policies and service development aimed at black and minority communities were virtually non-existent (Hughes and Bhaduri 1987, p.3). Around the time at which the Bill leading to the Act was in passage through Parliament, it was noted that 'Few Social Services Departments have made much progress in developing their services to minority communities and those that have are little advanced' (Watt and Cook 1989, p.74).

There was little or no demand for services from the Black communities at that time in the town refered to except for requests for practical help with equipment and adaptations, so the onus was on the social services department to take the initiative. It took a great deal of time to arrive at an agreed strategy to develop service provision, not least because our ambition of reaching consensus with a number of community organisations proved to be unrealistic. Another influential and time-consuming factor was the political pressures and influences from outside the communities, which came to play a decisive role. Throughout our work with minority ethnic communities, we have tried to adhere to a model of partnership and user participation. The challenges of managing imbalances of power in this model, and attempts to overcome these, proved complex and, again, time-consuming. However, the result has been the achievement of some services specifically designed for Black communities. Some important lessons have been learned, which will help us in building on the foundations that have been laid.

The context for service development

Warwickshire's minority ethnic populations reside mainly in three localities. The focus of this chapter is on one of these localities and in particular a town with a population of about 120,000 people, of whom just under 4 per cent are defined as from a minority ethnic background and of these just under 75 per cent are of Indian origin. (See Table 3.1.)

Table 3.1 Minority ethnic population profile	
Total population	117,048
Total minority ethnic population	4570 (3.9%)
of which: Black	425 (9.3%)
Indian	3380 (74.0%)
Other Asian	507 (11.1%)
Other	258 (5.6%)

Source: 1991 Census

The age profile of the minority ethnic population is younger than the rest of the population with only 3.5 per cent of pensionable age compared with 16.1 per cent of the total population. However, the number of people of pensionable age from the minority ethnic population is set to increase over the coming years. The significance of this is in the fact that by far the largest group of users of social services is older people (over 65 years) who account for 75 per cent of new referrals.

Another characteristic of the local minority ethnic population is its diversity, with a relatively high number of community organisations, reflecting primarily different religious denominations in communities of Indian origin. The largest group is Muslim, with a number of organisations reflecting different religions and social or cultural interests. The other groups of Indian origin are Sikh and Hindu. There is also a small African-Caribbean population. In addition, there are organisations which do not represent a particular religious group but instead represent specific interests, such as women's interests, or have a more general concern with welfare. These local groups are very keen to maintain their own identities and represent their own interests. There is no Race Equality Council (unlike the other two localities in Warwickshire with significant minority ethnic populations) and no collective body to represent the groups' interests. From the outset, there was a high level of political awareness in these groups and a strong ambition to secure resources to develop facilities for each community organisation so that general social, cultural and religious needs could be addressed. A particular focus for most groups was the acquisition and development of their own community centres.

When the work began in the early 1990s, the social services department had very few users from the minority ethnic communities and had no specialist provision catering for them. This was reflected in a lack of apparent demand for services, as seen in the very low number of referrals. This in turn deprived the department of a valuable source of information about needs, namely, feedback from current users of services. At the time, there was no other source of information about the needs of the minority ethnic communities, and a lack of experience with and knowledge of them. The converse was equally true. The communities had little or no experience of the social services department, its functions, services and priorities.

In this situation, one of the key catalysts for change – alongside the commitment of staff from local agencies and voluntary organisations – was the arrival of a new Director of Social Services in 1992. He had a strong and well-publicised commitment to race equality and the leadership that he provided gave a significant impetus and support to the work described in this chapter. The role of the leader is critical in changing an organisation's culture, principally through the support s/he gives to its core values and ideas, which are then incorporated into the organisation's structures and systems. The Director initiated developments in the department at this time including a strategy and procedures for race equality, and a ring-fenced budget for service development, which strengthened the contextual support for our work. This high level of commitment within the social services department came as a welcome opportunity for local staff to start afresh in addressing issues of race equality. This fresh start coincided with the introduction of assessment and care management, following the implementation of the National Health Service and Community Care Act (1990), which presented the chance to develop services in a new way: needs-led and user-led. Coupled with the acknowledgement by the almost exclusively white staff of their lack of experience and knowledge of the needs of the Black communities, this led to an approach based on partnership. By partnership, we mean engaging with, and encouraging the participation of, the Black communities in the planning, development and delivery of services to meet their needs, in a way that had not been tried with the majority white community up to that point.

Another significant change in the context for our work was a changing political environment in which support from district and county councillors for the minority ethnic communities became more apparent. There was a growing political consciousness among the Black community leaders and an ability and willingness to engage political support from councillors, which helped to overcome some of the power imbalance between the community leaders and the social services department. This helped to make the principle of partnership more genuine, rather than it becoming somewhat tokenistic which can be the outcome if there is a marked imbalance of power between the partners.

The final aspect of the changing context was the decision of the social services department to create an 'ethnic minority development budget', which could only be used for the development of services for Black communities. It was initially set at £60,000 for our locality and was subsequently increased in line with inflation. Unfortunately, it became a source of some fairly bitter contention, primarily between the social services department and the Black communities, but also among the different community groups who were all anxious to obtain a share of the resources. (It has been observed elsewhere that funding which is specifically set aside for 'special provision' for minority ethnic communities can lead to competition for resources on the basis of 'culturally distinctive needs' (Husband 1996; Walker and Ahmad 1994; Watters 1995)). The community leaders saw the budget as 'theirs' by right and asked that it be divided among them. It came to be regarded as a capital budget to develop the infrastructure of the organisations in the form of community centres, rather than as a revenue budget for services. This view was reinforced by the early emphasis – agreed by the social services department and the community organisations – on developing infrastructure in the form of bases from which services could be delivered. In this way, a mismatch of expectations was created about the priority and focus for service development, in that the priority for the community groups was to develop their general infrastructure to meet social, cultural and religious needs, whereas for social services the priority was the delivery of community care services. This mismatch of expectations persisted throughout the period described in this chapter.

Having elaborated the context in which our work took place, the remainder of the chapter discusses how it progressed by dividing its development into a series of stages, each of which is considered in turn. The first four stages provide the historical backdrop to the development of services for

Black communities. The remaining stages provide insight into the issues and dynamics of working in partnership with communities, within a politically charged and sensitive environment.

Stage one: making contact

The initial aim was to try to overcome the lack of contact and knowledge that the local agencies had of the minority ethnic communities. This was approached on a multi-agency basis. A working group was established with representatives from the Council for Voluntary Service, district council, police, and health, community education and social services. The group decided to organise three sessions which were intended to provide information about the work of the agencies and to establish a dialogue about the ways in which services could be tailored to meet the needs of the Black communities. The sessions ran throughout the day and into the evening. The daytime was used as a drop-in event with displays of information and staff and interpreters on hand to answer questions. The evening was more structured, with presentations from agency representatives on specific themes, followed by a general discussion. The sessions were well attended and well received, although attendance reduced rather than increased over the three sessions. They were useful in breaking down some barriers and establishing communication. Although the discussions were on too general a level to enable service planning, two key issues emerged which needed to be addressed.

First, it was clear that the minority ethnic communities, understandably, had very limited knowledge of the central tasks and priorities of the different agencies. For example, the main priority for the community leaders was to develop facilities to meet the social, cultural and religious needs of their members. This did not coincide with the specific community care priorities of the social services department and this provided obvious potential for the mismatch of expectations referred to in the previous section. A second issue to emerge was that dialogue with the communities was through their leaders, with little opportunity to discuss service planning in a more general way with other members of the communities, including potential service users and their carers. (This has been seen as a commonly encountered issue when attempting to establish links between social services departments and minority ethnic communities (Watt and Cooke 1989, p.82)).

Stage two: developing dialogue

One specific action, which followed on from Stage One, was the decision to appoint a Community Liaison Officer, funded from Joint Finance[1], for a period of two years. Community leaders were involved in the selection process. They agreed the job specification, met with the candidates and had a representative on the interview panel.

It was decided that the post would be based at, and supervised by, the Council for Voluntary Service in order to emphasise the independence of the role and to avoid the person appointed being seen as 'a social services person'. The main tasks for the Community Liaison Officer were to:

- research the needs of the minority ethnic communities

- inform commissioners and providers in health and social services of service development requirements

- improve communication and mutual understanding between the communities and the agencies.

A steering group was established to give advice and guidance to the post with representatives from each of the main Black community organisations and from health and social services and the Council for Voluntary Service. This met regularly throughout the duration of the post and provided an invaluable, though challenging, opportunity to debate proposals for a strategy to meet the social care needs of the Black communities.

There were some serious difficulties for the post-holder. Basing the post at the Council for Voluntary Service turned out to be a mistake as it served to create confusion about the role. This in turn led to a lack of credibility and acceptance of the post by the community leaders. It also led to difficulties in communication and accountability. On the positive side the post served as a stimulus for a great deal of discussion between community leaders and the social services department. Information about the community care needs of the minority ethnic communities was produced and this enabled an initial strategy for the development of services to be formulated. The strategy took account of two key factors: the relatively small number of people likely to be eligible for services because of the size and age distribution of the Black communities and the large number of community organisations. The needs that had been identified pointed to the requirement for community-based support for older people and their carers, for example, day care, meals and home care. The aim which was promoted by the social services department was to develop initially a single service for the Black communities to provide day care, meals, and information and advice. This could then act as a focal point for the further identification of needs and the development of more specialist services.

One of the community organisations, which promoted itself as non-religious, non-political and non-sectarian, was already operating an advice and drop-in centre on a small scale. The centre was based in a community education building in the central part of the town. The organisation was keen to expand and develop its service to all of the communities. This proposal was put to the steering group. It was rejected by most of the community leaders. Although many accepted the arguments in favour of the proposal that was being put forward, they would only support it if it were in addition to funding for their own communities to develop services specific to their own needs.

In addition, the 'ethnic minority development budget' was still seen by the communities as 'their' money and they were insistent on each having a share of it. Their support for a 'single service' of the type being proposed was conditional on it being funded from another source. The possibility of funding from Joint Finance was explored but was not successful. In any event the proposed single service was not viable, as each community still wanted its own service. A further complication was that the organisation running the advice and drop-in centre was unacceptable to most of the community leaders, as they questioned its credibility and ability to deliver an appropriate service across the range of communities.

An alternative proposal was developed, which was that social services would take over responsibility for running and developing the service from the community education building. This would have overcome the objections to the particular organisation in the original proposal, but this proposal foundered on the unwillingness of community leaders to forego their share of the development budget. In the end each organisation was allocated a small grant, except for the organisation running the advice and drop-in service which received a larger grant to reflect the work it had done in already having developed a service which was in accordance with the social services department's intended strategy.

We had arrived at something of a stalemate, with some fundamental differences of opinion about how to proceed. The social services view at operational level was that it was impractical to have as a starting point the development by each community of its own separate service. This position was based on the relatively small numbers who would be eligible for a service, the lack of experience of most of the community groups as service providers and the wish to promote services which were as inclusive as possible: a position in conflict with the model of separate services for separate communities. Thus, there was a difference of values between the social services department and the community leaders, as well as a different set of priorities. The department prioritised community care as opposed to the more general development of the community groups' infrastructure and resources for religious, cultural and social needs.

Stage three: developing in-house services

While progress was slow in service developments outside the social services department, attention was being given simultaneously to in-house services in order to make them more responsive to the needs of Black communities. In particular, the aim was to develop a flexible service through recruitment of a small team of Black workers who could work across different settings, including home care, respite – both home and residentially based – and long-term residential care. There was only limited success in recruiting Black staff, despite extensive efforts to publicise posts in the local minority ethnic communities, offers of help with completion of application forms and offering work placements to Black students. One of the reasons appeared to be the low status attached to personal care work.

The refurbishment of the social services department's local residential home for older people presented an opportunity to engage with community leaders in discussion about development of in-house services in general and specifically to consult them about the refurbishment plans. Community leaders were invited to meetings at the home. The plans were inspected and discussed and modifications were made to reflect cultural and religious needs. These were mainly concerned with the needs of Muslim users, such as the alignment of the toilets and the hand-washing facilities. A multi-denominational prayer-room was included. Once assurances had been given that the refurbishment and the development of the in-house services were to be funded from mainstream budgets, and not the 'ethnic minority development budget', this proved to be a valuable exercise both in giving information about mainstream services and in generating much goodwill following the period of difficult negotiations in Stage Two.

At the conclusion of the time-limited Community Liaison Officer post, the social services department decided that it would create a permanent Ethnic Minority Liaison Officer who would be employed by social services. The role of this post was to develop communication between the social services department and the Black communities and to advise on and assist with the development of services.

Stage four: agreeing a new strategy

There was a great deal of political activity by the community leaders who sought support from councillors and other politically active Black people in the county to resolve the impasse with the department, referred to at the end of Stage Two. This put pressure on the Director of Social Services to come up with a resolution. His intervention resulted in a new strategy. He rejected suggestions from within the locality's social services that the way forward, for an interim period of up to five years, was for social services to be the main provider of services to meet the community care needs of the Black communities. This proposal was put forward from the local social services team in recognition of the difficulty which the local community organisations would have in becoming service providers and so that work could be undertaken with them to develop their capacity to take on service provision, if they wished to do so. Some of the development budget would have been used to employ specialist care managers to work with the minority ethnic communities.

Instead, the new strategy that the Director of Social Services decided on and agreed with the community leaders was that the department would purchase services from local community groups, if they wished to be providers, and that help would be provided to enable them to take on this role. The alternative was that the social services department would be the provider for specific communities, in partnership with them. As it would clearly have been impossible to implement this strategy at the same time with all of the communities, a system of prioritisation was agreed whereby the largest communities would be addressed first, with smaller communities following on in subsequent years. The Muslim community formed the largest group and there was an agreement that the various Muslim community groups would work together in developing services for their whole community.

Stage five: implementation of the new strategy

In order to make working in partnership a reality, it was essential for social services in the locality to address three main issues:

- The Black communities were diverse.
- The 'ethnic minority development budget' was small.
- Providing limited funding to the diverse community groups wanting an allocation from the budget would lead to fragmented provision.

The social services department acknowledged the diversity within the Black communities and was careful not to favour one group over another. However, it was impossible to fund each of the minority ethnic groups separately as the 'ethnic minority development budget' was very limited and there was no offer of releasing any of the department's mainstream funding. The communities saw the 'ethnic minority development budget' as capital funding which should be spent on providing community venues from which services would be run. The department on the other hand did not attach specific long-term criteria to the fund and social services in the locality perceived the funding as start-up monies for providing the services themselves. The only other pot of mainstream funding available was from the low priority budget. This budget was funding that the department ring-fenced for projects and services that did not fit with the department's priority areas, but were perceived by the department as providing valuable preventive services. Furthermore, even if each of the groups had received funding, it would have led to fragmented provision. To find a way forward the department entered into a dialogue with the community representatives. The community organisations developed alliances from which emerged four major organisations, each one serving a specific religious and cultural Black community:

- the Muslim Organisation – comprised of representatives from all of the Muslim organisations
- the Hindu Organisation – representing the Hindu communities
- the Caribbean Organisation – representing the African-Caribbean communities
- the Sikh Organisation – representing the Sikh communities.

The agreement was that these four major organisational groupings would be active partners in the planning and development of services, representing the needs of their respective groups – Muslim, Hindu, African-Caribbean and Sikh. The understanding was that members of the other smaller groups would have equal access to the services provided by these organisations. This meant that members of the other smaller Muslim religious, social and cultural groups would have 'equal' access to the services provided by the major Muslim organisation with whom they had formed an alliance. The Hindu, Sikh and Caribbean organisations also had similar agreements with their own respective smaller partners. Although the services being developed were targeted towards meeting the needs of each of the organisational groupings' respective communities, they were not perceived as exclusive to these communities. In fact, the criterion set by the department, which was agreed by the communities, was that in order to offer choice to the potential users, the services would consider users from across the 'Asian communities' although priority would be given to members of the respective communities. This agreement was vital as it prevented further fragmentation of services to the communities.

Stage six: development of the partnership model

The social services department was already engaged in a dialogue with the community leaders on identifying service priorities. Through this process, the need to develop services for older members of their communities was seen as a priority by all of the steering groups established to develop services. (The African-Caribbean community also identified the need to prioritise services for children and young people.)

The representatives from the four organisational groupings on the steering groups charged with developing services were individuals, mainly men, who were perceived by the social services department as having been elected by their respective communities to represent them. As such, the representation on the steering groups reflected the make-up of the management committees of the four major organisational groupings. The management committees of volunteer members, the majority of whom were male, were elected annually by their respective memberships in the small community organisations. They were elected to the executive positions year on year and thus established themselves as 'leaders' of their communities. These leaders were also involved in a number of other groups and committees representing their communities. The statutory agencies perceived them as the voices of, and gatekeepers to, their communities and therefore regarded them as important partners. They were also perceived as having the grass-roots knowledge of the social and health care needs within their communities. The inclusion of these representatives on the steering groups, in addition to social services operational managers and the Ethnic Minority Liaison Officer, was viewed as an essential step towards forging effective partnerships. This approach was successful in empowering the community representatives by involving them as equal players in setting the agenda for the development of services which were culturally sensitive, accessible and appropriate to their communities.

However, as the meetings of the steering groups progressed, it became apparent that the community leaders had their own agendas. The community leaders were not necessarily fully representing the issues and concerns of users and carers and there was a need for separate user and carer voices on these groups. The community representatives were coming up with lists of names of potential users, but the social services department had very little information about the overall needs of the older members from these communities. This left us with a dilemma of whether to continue depending solely on the existing representatives or whether to adopt another approach. The result was a two-pronged approach. We continued to engage with the community representatives and explored the possibility of developing a user perspective through the involvement of potential users. The social services department developed an action research study to gather information about the community care needs of the minority ethnic population and piloted a user focus group initiative to begin involving users. The aims of these projects were:

- to provide the necessary information on the existing and future needs of the older people and adults with disabilities in the Black communities

- to consult with potential service users and carers on the development of services

- to use the research as a catalyst to develop a user forum.

Stage seven: action research study

The social services department wanted to make the research process both participatory and anti-oppressive. The organisations were asked to encourage interested community members to apply for the positions of sessional research / outreach workers. These posts were also advertised extensively on Asian radio and through the local Black voluntary sector. We were conscious that each community wanted at least one researcher from their own community and there were no applications from the African-Caribbean community. As a result, we proceeded with the study only in relation to the Asian communities.

Four researchers were recruited, each having knowledge of one or more of the Asian cultures in the town. In addition, each of them spoke one or more Asian languages. The methodology used was individual interviews based on a questionnaire. Community representatives referred lists of potential users who became the immediate sample for the study. The researchers identified additional participants for the study through their outreach contacts with the participants, their own knowledge of the communities and their contact with other members of the communities. The research provided information on:

- user and carer perceptions of the social services department and its services
- views on service preference and delivery.

It helped to build a service needs profile of the respective communities and identified gaps in service provision. It also provided access to a group of individuals who were willing to participate in a focus group. The research provided some views on service delivery which were different from those of the community leaders. The majority of participants felt that the most important elements in providing a service which they would want to access were staff awareness and respect of their religious, cultural and dietary needs. They also indicated a high preference for staff able to speak their language but they did not consider it crucial that the provider organisation or its staff should be from their own religion and/or community. Although overwhelming support was voiced for specialist services for minority ethnic communities, participants also wanted to have a choice between mainstream and specialist services.

The action research study was a useful starting point in entering a dialogue with individuals who would potentially require community care services. To extend further its commitment to engaging with potential service users, the social services department backed the Ethnic Minority Liaison Officer's recommendation to pilot a 'user forum initiative'. Some of the participants from the research study volunteered to take part in a user forum and explore the possibility of becoming involved in the department's consultation process and in the development of the services being planned.

An independent advocate was commissioned to provide user empowerment training and facilitate a session with the user group. The focus group highlighted a number of key issues for the social services department. These were as follows:

- The participants had very little knowledge about social services and did not distinguish social services from health services or social security.

- There was very little knowledge in the group about the initiatives and developments on which the department was embarking.

- Concerns were raised about the role of community representatives in 'passing on the message' and representing them.

- The participants wanted to be involved in the service development discussions and wanted the department to regard them as equal partners.

- The participants wanted to have further sessions involving more people from their communities with a view to setting themselves up as a separate consultation panel.

The focus group pilot added to the information already gathered through the research project. It gave a clear message that the consultation and partnership with the community leaders should not be perceived as the only avenue through which the developments would become a reality. The potential users and their carers wanted to be part of this partnership and wanted to be heard. The research and focus group exercise also highlighted the need to improve in-house services and to make them more accessible and appropriate to the needs of the diverse minority ethnic population.

Stage eight: voluntary versus mainstream

The social services department, encouraged by the information gathered from the two initiatives discussed above, moved ahead. The two organisations which now pushed on with their developments were the Hindu Organisation and the Muslim Organisation. Both wanted to develop day care services. The Hindu day care project is a voluntary sector service directly managed by the Hindu Organisation and funded by the social services department. The Muslim project is the first specialist mainstream service developed, funded and delivered by Nuneaton and Bedworth Social Services using the Muslim Organisation's premises. Both developments presented major challenges and highlighted key issues in partnership working.

The Hindu project

The Hindu Organisation was a voluntary organisation that had been established for a few years. The organisation provided a range of religious and social activities, including a social club for its older members. It had achieved charitable status and had secured a lottery bid to purchase and refurbish a building for community use. The management committee underestimated the cost of completing this centre and entered into negotiations with the social services department to secure additional funds. They wanted to develop educational, cultural and religious services for the Hindu community and the provision of community care services for their older members was part of this vision.

The social services department regarded the day care project as representing a number of valuable opportunities. These included:

- the existence of a willing and enthusiastic minority ethnic service provider

- access to older members from the Hindu community

- the opportunity to develop a partnership approach which allowed the Hindu community to be an equal and influential partner.

To develop the day care service, the social services department set up a project steering group comprising representatives from the organisation's management committee and from the department. The objective of the steering group was to agree the way forward. The initial discussions revolved mainly around the financial shortfall the organisation had to meet in order to get its newly purchased building to an operational standard. These discussions continued without any firm decision as to the funding the department was prepared to agree. It was acknowledged that the discussions about funding the building would delay the development of day care, a service much needed within the community. The organisation shared this concern and a joint decision was taken to begin the development of the service by situating it temporarily within the community centre already frequented by the elders of the community.

Contract negotiations with the organisation led to an agreement that the social services department would purchase twelve day care places. The Service Level Agreement included specific standards of service delivery and stated that the involvement of users and carers should be seen as intrinsic to the progress of the service. In light of this expectation, the arrangements for the steering group were reviewed to include user representation.

The progress from this initial planning to the realisation of the service took one year. Major challenges faced, and overcome, on the way included:

- recognising and addressing the fact that although the organisation had the enthusiasm and commitment to become a direct provider, it lacked the organisational capacity and skills to do so

- a real concern that we could be setting up a service to 'fail'

- problems related, on the one hand, to operating an 'open access' service which involved the department buying a number of day care places for users who met its criteria and, on the other hand, allowing the organisation to accept other users who were considered to need day care, but who did not meet the department's usual criteria

- the tenuous relationship between the organiser of the new day care service and the management committee; the organiser was appointed to manage the day care project, but found herself taking a back seat as all the major decisions on access and activity development were being made and implemented by management committee representatives on the steering group.

To address these issues, the social services department commissioned capacity building training for all members of the organisation's management committee. The participants also included those members of the committee who had been nominated onto the steering group, which was set up to plan the service developments. The training gave them an overview of their responsibilities as employers and service providers. Follow-on advice and support was given to the committee and the organiser by the department's Ethnic Minority Liaison Officer. This went some way towards resolving some of the issues and provided the committee with valuable information and knowledge.

As the service became operational, the department's staff assessed all of the potential service users. Those who met the department's eligibility criteria were allocated a place. Those who did not meet the department's criteria had the option of being assessed by the day care service organiser. This meant that they could access the day care with the agreement of the management committee and the organiser (open access route). The open access route was necessary because social services departments tend to develop service access criteria from a 'Euro-centric perspective' which ignores the needs of Black and minority ethnic service users. A key assumption in this perspective is that 'Black communities look after their own' through an extended family network. Such an assumption ignores the needs of potential Black users who might be living within extended families, but who do not have the support of their families during the day and could be as vulnerable at those times as white people living on their own.

This day care service operates three days a week, with a daily attendance of between 15 and 20.

The Muslim project

The Muslim communities in Nuneaton comprise several small groups, each having its own identity and organisational framework. Despite these traditional differences in the locality, all of these groups agreed to form a partnership in order to work with the social services department in moving ahead with developments. The largest group, the Muslim Society, owned a building and took the lead in the negotiations with the department. The rest of the groups were represented on the steering group which planned the service.

The building owned by the major Muslim group is in the heart of the Muslim community and was a suitable venue for the delivery of services. The department viewed the Muslim service development as an opportunity to gain knowledge and experience in developing mainstream specialist provision and substantial funding was provided to refurbish the Centre. A systematic approach was used in achieving the Muslim service development. The department hoped to provide a range of services from the Centre including mobile meals and day care. Although the representatives of the Muslim communities highlighted services for older people as a priority, the department also wanted to explore the development of children's services, which it felt was as important and needed by the community. The community leadership supported the department in this, but indicated that service development for older people was the priority. A number of planning and partnership groups were established. These were:

- a steering group comprising social services staff and representatives from all the Muslim groups

- a management group comprising the district ethnic minority liaison officer, adult team manager, home care manager, the district service development officer and a residential care home manager

- practitioner planning groups comprising social workers, day service and residential workers from the various adult service areas looking at specific developments.

The aim of establishing these groups was to get a wide perspective and ownership for the project. The research and focus group pilot, referred to earlier, provided us with user views on the planning and delivery of the services.

The Muslim Community Centre was officially launched but turned out to be far from suitable for the provision of a range of services. We had failed to make specifications clear about what facilities would be needed and the result was that we had a large hall, which was only suitable for community events. As a result, the 'premises issue' was continuously on the agenda of the community steering group and the social services department's management group. This prolonged discussion and, along with other difficulties we encountered in the partnership, delayed the launch of the services by 15 months. Some of the major problems we encountered were:

- the difficulties of working with several interest groups, each with a strong identity

- the other interests of the Muslim organisation; it was accessing European funding to extend the premises further and turn the Centre into a training provider

- the smaller Muslim groups feeling excluded from the discussions and worrying that their members would not get access to the services

- that fact that, within the social services department, there was a lack of commitment from children's services to joining the partnership, resulting in the developments being based only around adult services

- that fact that the senior management within the social services locally did not seem to recognise the difficulties that we were encountering; this meant that they could not offer the appropriate and necessary support to the operational managers and the Ethnic Minority Liaison Officer who were in the forefront of the developments

- the issues of premises and priorities over how, when and what should be provided which dragged on for months

- our failure to clarify the role of the steering group through clear terms of reference which resulted in meetings being poorly attended and becoming a time for the community representatives to complain about social services staff

- the staff getting roped into the arguments at the expense of making firm decisions on the service delivery aspects.

The Muslim community was becoming dissatisfied with the lack of progress. The message given to the community by their leadership was that the social services department was 'dragging its feet' and being 'uncooperative'. This perception slowly changed through the experience of the research study and the focus group pilot in which participants were brought up to date with the issues and developments. These participants then passed the information through to the Muslim community. The practitioner group was frustrated because it had carried out all of the groundwork in its specific areas. The outcome was a loss of interest, with most of the practitioner group disappearing, never to emerge again. The management group also shared the feelings of frustration. However, the commitment and drive of this group kept the project alive.

In order to overcome these major challenges, the social services department reviewed the situation and developed an action plan with targets and timescales for the completion of the various stages of development. The steering group stopped meeting for a while and the department began a direct dialogue with the key player and owner of the building to resolve the issue of premises. A crucial development was the recruitment of a co-ordinator who played a vital role within the community in progressing the Muslim project. The community leaders engaged constructively in trying to solve the problems.

Under the terms of the plan of action, a service for older Muslim women was developed and located at a social services in-house venue. The services began to materialise slowly and eventually moved into the Muslim Community Centre. The day care provision is currently available four days a week and there is a mobile meal service for the housebound. There are still limitations on what can be provided from the Centre, owing to its physical suitability, and there are still unresolved issues around funding and other developments. However, the achievement of the existing specialist services, despite the obstacles, provides the drive and enthusiasm for making the partnership continue to work.

Conclusion

The developments we have described were consistent with the social services department's commitment to meeting the Commission for Racial Equality's *Racial Equality means Quality Standard for Local Government* (CRE 1995). The *Standard* provided a range of performance criteria for race equality and departments were asked to develop action plans with targets for employment and service delivery. Nuneaton and Bedworth district's locality's approach was to ask every unit and service to produce a Race Equality Action Plan with specific, measurable and achievable targets to improve their services and increase the number of Black staff within the workforce.

However, the journey towards race equality in access to services has been difficult and an uphill struggle at times. The approaches we have used have taught us some valuable lessons. We would like to share this learning with practitioners and agencies embarking on a similar journey. The lessons we learnt were:

- to recognise that Black and minority ethnic communities are not homogenous; they are diverse in language, religion, culture, needs and aspirations

- to be aware of the impact of policies and practices such as service access criteria that disproportionately disadvantage these communities and thus are discriminatory

- to build a current and future service needs profile of the communities

- to develop both short-term and long-term strategies that address the needs of these diverse communities

- to identify and make available adequate financial resources needed for sustaining these services

- to review current mainstream provision with rigour and make it more responsive to the needs of the diverse population

- to develop a commitment from the top to the bottom of the organisation in the pursuit of race equality

- to analyse the local political environment within which race equality operates

- to clarify expectations at the outset of entering into any partnership

- to clarify and state terms of reference for any partnership group

- to assure the active involvement of users and carers within the partnership

- to be flexible and adaptable to the changing and emerging agendas

- to provide capacity building to Black and minority ethnic voluntary organisations.

We have not sought to provide a perfect model of partnership in progressing race equality. What we have attempted to demonstrate is that taking race equality seriously is challenging and requires tenacity, but is ultimately rewarding. The combination of approaches we have used has given us the basis from which to build and progress developments in our locality. One of the knock-on effects we have seen is that, for the first time, we are able to recruit Black staff into our home care and residential care services. This has resulted in a small but significant increase in uptake of these services.

Note

1 Joint Finance is a joint budget of health and social services monies which is used to provide short-term funding for innovative schemes.

Chapter Four

Working with Health

From Collaboration to Partnership in a Hospital Setting

Carol Roy and Eileen Watts

Introduction

The Department of Health's *Modernising Social Services* (1998a) and *Partnership in Action* (1998b) set out clear expectations that social services departments and the National Health Service would be involved jointly – to a far greater extent than previously – in strategic planning, service commissioning and service provision. Such expectations had clear implications for the practice of social workers based in acute hospital teams. In these settings, collaboration with health care workers is an everyday necessity if the best services possible are to be provided for service users. A fifth of all social workers employed by social services departments are hospital-based, rendering them a crucial point of access to social work services (McLeod and Bywaters 2000, p.101). Hospital social work is therefore a key site for the exploration of the possibilities of collaborative working and partnership with health professionals (Bywaters and McLeod 1996; McLeod and Bywaters 2000).

This chapter traces the development of the emphasis on collaboration between health and social services. It provides an account of collaborative working with health professionals on four jointly planned projects: Halfway Home, Responsive Emergency Assessment Care Team (REACT), Winter Pressures Group and Palliative Care Group. The benefits and constraints of collaborative working are considered by drawing on these examples from the work of social workers in a hospital team. The chapter concludes by reviewing current trends in government policy for health and social services, which call for a shift from collaboration to partnership.

Community care and social work in hospital settings

The community care reforms and health/social services collaboration

In 1986 the Audit Commission highlighted problems of fragmentation and poor co-ordination between health and social services as constraints on the development of community care (Audit Commission 1986). As was discussed in Chapter One, following this report Sir Roy Griffiths was commissioned by the government to undertake a review of how public funds were spent in support of community care policies and to advise on how the funds might be used more effectively (Griffiths 1988). Griffiths' mandate was focused primarily on four groups of adults: older people, people with mental ill health, people with physical disabilities and people with learning disabilities. These groups required 'more than the usual care and support from others' (Griffiths 1988, p.3). In providing this care and support, Griffiths emphasised the need for joint planning and action between health and social services at a local level (Griffiths 1988, p.16). He stressed the need for health and social services to provide greater clarity regarding responsibility and accountability for plans and actions involved in providing community care services. He highlighted the need for particular attention to be paid to services at the direct point of delivery and for precision in the implementation of certain key elements in health and social services joint plans (Griffiths 1988, p.16), namely:

- identification and assessment of need
- consultation with carers and those being cared for
- design of care packages
- setting priorities
- monitoring.

The majority of Griffiths' proposals filtered through into the White Paper, *Caring for People* (1989). This re-emphasised the need for working collaboratively as the basis for the provision of a 'seamless service' to those people with health and social care needs. The aim was to improve the co-ordination of the provision of community care services for those people with complex care needs. In consultation with service users, carers and families, a multi-agency assessment was envisaged with a jointly planned care package designed to meet service users' specific needs. Via this White Paper, the essential elements of the Griffiths Report (1988) became law in the National Health Service and Community Care Act (1990). The Act underlined once again the responsibilities of health and social services to develop community care together in a 'seamless service' for service users and carers. The partnership between health and social services was reinforced in the guidance on the implementation of the Act, which set out the significance of health care as an 'integral part of community care' in the joint planning of services (Social Services Inspectorate 1991b, p.83). This was part and parcel of a flurry of government policy and practice guidance which advocated various models of assessment and care management, with a strong emphasis on multi-disciplinary and multi-agency working which demanded that professionals 're-think their approach to arranging and providing care' (Social Services Inspectorate 1991a, p.7). The organisational changes which resulted from the community care reforms demanded a reassessment of traditional relationships among different professional groups and agencies (Phillipson 1992, p.1).

New Labour and health/social services collaboration

The Labour government, elected in 1997, conveyed a strong desire to see traditional barriers between health and social services removed in the interests of providing more efficient and effective services (Department of Health 1998a, 1998b, 1998c). A number of themes run through the Department of Health's papers which point to the key role which social workers are expected to play in developing strategies to implement government policies. First, health and social services should demonstrate an ability to work more collaboratively. Second, services from both authorities should meet the needs of patients/service users at the strategic level through joint planning in localities and at the individual level by direct provision of services to meet health and social care needs. Third, social services should work with health services to reduce unnecessary admissions to hospital. Fourth, joint efforts should be made to provide appropriate placements for patients/service users after their discharge from hospital.

These themes strike a chord with our experience. 'Social admissions' of older people, an aspect of the third theme, account for a significant proportion of the referrals that we receive as hospital social workers. These can be, for example, the result of an older person having had a fall. No real injury is sustained but the person feels traumatised and has nobody at home to care for them. Another example is admission as a consequence of the illness of a carer. There have been some jointly funded schemes between health and social services to prevent social admissions to hospital. These include rapid emergency response teams which assess a person's needs either in the community or in the accident and emergency department and provide initial care packages. Another example is emergency night sitting services. The government is keen to see further development of such schemes throughout the country (Department of Health 1998b, p.16).

In relation to the fourth theme, poor discharge planning can often result in readmission to hospital much to the distress of service users and carers: 'Discharge from hospital can be a major life event for both user and carer. It also has substantial implications for the best use of both health and social care resources. Good quality discharge should not be a matter of chance' (Department of Health 1994b, p.1). Some hospital discharges fail when there has not been a full multi-disciplinary discharge planning meeting for those with complex needs; or where a person assessed by nursing staff as having simple needs is discharged to their home and has to wait for a full assessment (Social Services Inspectorate 1998). Improvement in hospital discharge has been noted when social workers are hospital-based (Social Services Inspectorate 1998) and when hospital trusts have a dedicated discharge co-ordinator and 'hospital at home' schemes (Department of Health 1998b).

These sorts of developments are indicative of greater collaboration between health and social services. However, there has been one other initiative to encourage further joined-up work – the pooling of budgets (Department of Health 1998b). With the implementation of the Health Act (1999), pooled budgets will encourage much stronger and more formal partnership arrangements between health and social services (Community Care April 2000, pp.20–21).

Against this backcloth, the next section outlines four collaborative ventures between health and social services which attempted to work with the policy exhortations to engage in collaborative approaches. The ventures are:

- Halfway Home: a rehabilitation unit to prepare patients for discharge

- Winter Pressures Group: a multi-disciplinary team which addresses the added pressures on services during the winter months

- Responsive Emergency Assessment Care Team (REACT): a rapid assessment service for people in emergency situations

- Palliative Care Group: a multi-disciplinary team which addresses the special needs of people who are terminally ill.

Four collaborative ventures

Halfway Home

The litmus test in debates about the efficacy of hospital-based social work has often been the contribution it has made to planning discharges (McLeod and Bywaters 2000, p.95). Acute hospital services are obliged to operate efficiently and contain costs, and 'bed-blocking' is the antithesis of these objectives. Hence the constant pressure on 'freeing' beds to make room for new admissions (Connolly 1997, p.297). The pressure to speed up 'patient throughput', coupled with under-funded social services departments' focus on 'core business', have combined to pressurise hospital social work to concentrate increasingly on swiftly executed discharge planning (McLeod and Bywaters 2000, p.97). In this context, delayed discharges are problematic. They may occur for several reasons. For example, a patient may require a complex care package in order to be able to return home; s/he may be awaiting placement in a residential or nursing home; s/he may have completed acute medical treatment but still require continuing rehabilitation.

In relation to the latter, the important roles rehabilitation services play, both in preventing inappropriate admission of older people to hospital and in facilitating their safe discharge home, have been recognised (Audit Commission 1997; Social Services Inspectorate 1998). Rehabilitation services benefit service users by helping to prevent hospital-acquired infection and enabling people to remain in their own homes or return to them. For health authorities rehabilitation services reduce the amount of time people spend in expensive in-patient beds (Audit Commission 1992b, p.30) and for social services departments such services can reduce the number of people entering residential and nursing home care to which they may well have to contribute funding. As these benefits of rehabilitation services were recognised, the government asked health and social services to develop a framework for multi-disciplinary assessment in community health and acute care settings and to establish a range of rehabilitation and recuperation facilities (Department of Health 1998b, p.16).

In response to these policy directions with regard to rehabilitation services, discussions began between health and social services with the aim of establishing a strategy to reduce delayed discharges from acute hospital beds through the development of a rehabilitation service. The outcome of those discussions was 'Halfway Home', a three-year project funded jointly by health and social services. The project remit was to continue rehabilitation and recovery and to reduce the level of dependency within 28 days. The project has two main aims: first, to facilitate prompt discharge from acute hospital beds through rehabilitation; second, to provide a multi-disciplinary approach to the discharge planning process. The project is nurse-led with support from specially trained care staff, physiotherapists and occupational therapists. Referral to Halfway Home is made by the social worker who has undertaken the initial assessment while a patient is on an acute ward.

A Project Board was established, comprising representatives from health and social services who included nurse managers, a clinical manager, social services managers, the senior hospital social worker and the project manager. At the beginning of the project, the Project Board met on a monthly basis to ensure that the Halfway Home remit was being met and to undertake any necessary alterations to its policies. (The project is now an established service within the hospital.)

Although based on the hospital site, it was agreed by the Project Board that Halfway Home would be given a homelier environment than that typically found on an acute hospital ward. Guests[1] would continue to share rooms, but they would be given more privacy. For example many of the rooms in Halfway Home have fewer beds than the acute wards. Guests have a wardrobe beside their bed in which to store their personal possessions and are encouraged to keep their own key to this. They have access to facilities not found on the acute wards, for example kitchen and dining areas. (The kitchen is also used as a rehabilitation assessment area.) They are encouraged to dress in their own clothes and to participate fully in the rehabilitation and discharge planning process.

The rehabilitation and discharge planning process commences at the initial assessment on the acute ward once the patient has agreed to a stay at Halfway Home. The social worker explains to the patient the roles of the physiotherapist, occupational therapist and nursing staff. S/he is made aware of the maximum length of the expected stay at Halfway Home and is informed about the multi-disciplinary pre-discharge planning meeting. Both patient and carer will be invited to this meeting so that self-perceived needs can be expressed. The hospital social work team is thus the gateway to the project, ensuring that referrals made to Halfway Home by acute nursing staff are appropriate. The patient must be in agreement with a stay at Halfway Home, s/he must have the potential to improve through rehabilitation and Halfway Home must not be the only option available to a patient, especially when staff are under pressure to free up an acute hospital bed.

The progress of each guest is discussed weekly at the multi-disciplinary team meeting. Members of this group include the clinical manager and/or staff nurse, care worker, physiotherapist, occupational therapist and hospital social worker. Social work attendance at this meeting is on a rotating basis, but the hospital social worker who is allocated to a particular guest remains involved with that guest throughout their stay. At this meeting agreement is reached on individual rehabilitation programmes and the guest's length of stay. This will have been discussed with the guest prior to the meeting. The maximum length of stay is 28 days. Before people are discharged to their home a full multi-disciplinary planning meeting is called to co-ordinate a guest's care package. Social workers involved in the project remain in contact with guests for six weeks following discharge, when the final review of the multi-disciplinary care package is undertaken. Ms A's experience of Halfway Home illustrates the centrality of multi-agency care packages in the approach adopted by the project.

MS A

Ms A was a 49-year-old woman admitted to hospital suffering from a degenerative respiratory disease. She was also disabled by curvature of the spine. Ms A's prognosis was very poor. The degenerative respiratory disease meant that she needed to use an oxygen cylinder constantly and, as a result, her mobility was extremely limited. She needed assistance with all personal care.

Following a full multi-disciplinary assessment, a number of factors came to light. Ms A's partner had a history of long-term mental ill health and her younger daughter had cerebral palsy. She used a wheelchair and attended a school for children with physical disabilities. The older daughter (16 years) had taken on the role of carer for the whole family. At the time of the assessment she felt depressed and was falling behind with her GCSE studies at school. She was considering getting engaged to her boyfriend, which she saw as a way out from what she experienced as her entrapment in the caring role.

Ms A. was referred to Halfway Home for recuperation following in-patient treatment for chronic respiratory disease. The recuperation and rehabilitation at Halfway Home also aimed to maximise her potential for mobility prior to discharge. This referral enabled the multi-disciplinary team to create a plan with Ms A. which would not only address her physical needs but would also address the needs of other family members.

A number of professionals were involved:

- The hospital social worker had already become involved, when Ms A was referred to the hospital.

- Social services home care became involved to provide care on discharge.

- A mental health social worker and community psychiatric nurse worked with Mr A.

- A community support worker from the mental health team also supported Mr A.

- Children's services were involved with the younger daughter, providing respite for her with foster carers.

- Counselling services were arranged to help the younger daughter to come to terms with her mother's condition and to deal with the mother's possible future needs.

- An educational psychologist became involved with the older daughter to help her see that responsibility for the whole family was not hers, and that she could offer support to her mother, father and sister without being the main carer.

- The district nurse provided support to Ms A mainly with respect to the management of medication and oxygen.

- Social services occupational therapists provided adaptations and aids within the home, thus making tasks which had previously been difficult easier for the family.

- As part of the discharge planning process a series of planning meetings were held which were facilitated by the social worker. All family members were invited and took an active part in the plans being made. It was important for everyone involved to see that planning for all family members was like a jigsaw, one part being dependent on the next. It was only by establishing a co-operative partnership and effective communication between agencies that a care package which met Ms A's specific needs was achieved.

- At the last multi-disciplinary review, the family were all functioning better than they had been before the crisis of Ms A's admission had necessitated multi-disciplinary action. Ms A's prognosis remains poor but she and the family are better able to understand and to come to terms with the outcome.

People at all levels in the hospital have been delighted by the success of Halfway Home. The project has greatly reduced delayed discharges from acute hospital beds. The emphasis on active and targeted rehabilitation has resulted in over 70 per cent of the Halfway Home guests (whose average age was 80 years) being discharged to their home.

There have been occasions when people destined for nursing homes have either returned to, or entered for the first time, residential care homes. This is largely due to Halfway Home having been able to provide a longer period to recuperate and active rehabilitation having promoted daily living skills. A further indicator of the success of Halfway Home is that members of the multi-disciplinary team have developed a better understanding of each other's roles. This has resulted from working so closely together, through in-house training organised by the clinical manager and through therapists who have transferred some of their skills to the nursing staff, thus ensuring a continuous process of rehabilitation rather than the shorter rehabilitation sessions given by individual therapists on acute wards. The Halfway Home team have developed greater insight into the contribution of the social work role.

The nursing staff have developed a different style of working with the guests in Halfway Home. First, the pace of work is much slower on Halfway Home than on the acute wards. Consequently, staff are able to spend more time with their guests. Second, they have learnt new techniques for motivating and stimulating guests. This has been achieved through encouraging participation in social activities such as reminiscence sessions and art and craft. Third, the staff have become more willing to allow guests to take risks and actively to encourage independence. Sometimes on acute wards it is quicker and safer to do things for the patient rather than allow them to do things for themselves.

Winter Pressures Group

'Winter pressures' is a term used to describe the excessive pressures experienced by acute hospital and community services during the winter months. Such pressures may result from, for example, influenza epidemics which dramatically weaken vulnerable groups such as older people. This can result in increased numbers of admissions to acute hospital beds which can have the knock-on effect of preventing people being admitted from waiting lists for planned surgical procedures and medical treatment. In these circumstances, emergency admissions to hospitals put a strain on social services departments, which are required to co-ordinate quick and safe hospital discharges through community care packages.

Central government has allocated monies to be used jointly by health and social services on local projects to enable 'winter pressures' to be managed more effectively. A local Winter Pressures Group was formed, as a collaborative venture at strategic planning level, with the aim of reducing the impact of winter pressures on hospital and community care services. This group comprised senior nurse managers from both the hospital and community health trusts, managers from the social services adult community team, senior managers from social services, senior hospital social workers, a senior manager from the ambulance service, a consultant from the accident and emergency department within the trust, and a senior nurse manager from the health authority. Based on past experiences and knowledge of the locality, the multi-agency professionals in the Winter Pressures Group shared their views on how they would like the central government money to be used. The group identified gaps in current service provision and put forward ideas for new projects that might meet service user/patient needs.

The majority of the projects were in the form of joint bids from health and social services. The Winter Pressures Group considered each bid and allocated government money to projects it considered would have the greatest impact. Between 1997 and 1999, winter pressure money funded several projects, notably, the Responsive Emergency Assessment Care Team (REACT, see below), which prevented emergency social admissions to hospital of adults, mainly older people; a night sitting service; and extra physiotherapy and occupational therapy hours in rehabilitation day services. However, once the 'winter pressures' money was exhausted, with the exception of REACT the other projects ceased to exist.

The Winter Pressures Group showed that a collaborative approach to strategic planning and service delivery was not only desirable but was also achievable. Through collaboration, this multi-agency group engendered mutual respect for each other's opinions among professionals. The group showed a willingness to co-operate at senior management level which sent positive signals to front-line managers and practitioners. There were also direct gains for service users. For example, evaluation of the night sitting service showed an extremely high take-up rate.

Responsive Emergency Assessment Care Team (REACT)

As highlighted above, the Responsive Emergency Assessment Care Team (REACT) was one of the projects to which government funding for meeting winter pressures was allocated. (REACT is no longer a project but is now an established service.) The main remit of the project was to prevent social admission of adults, mainly older people, to acute hospital beds and to provide a service which, instead, would maintain people within the community. The REACT team was specifically recruited to provide a multi-skilled approach to the assessment process and the delivery of social and health care.

REACT consisted of two project managers, both senior nurse managers, one from the hospital trust and the other from the community health trust. Two nurses and a social worker were the co-ordinators. The project managers had responsibility for managing the budget, staff recruitment, public relations and monitoring and evaluation of the project. The co-ordinators' roles were to assess and provide emergency services to users and carers, reviewing care packages, and multi-disciplinary and multi-agency liaison and training. In addition, a small group of experienced community staff were recruited, with training provided by the co-ordinators.

REACT began in January 1998 and was funded for three months, as a free-of-charge service. It was based in the trust's accident and emergency department. In the initial stages of the project, the project managers and co-ordinators invested time not only in developing the project but also in public relations promoting the image of REACT and encouraging its take-up. REACT was discussed and promoted with key groups of people, who were potential referrers: professionals within the trust, general practitioners, district nurses, and social services community adult teams.

REACT does exactly what its title suggests. The co-ordinators provide a rapid holistic assessment of a person's individual needs and an intensive care package to meet those needs. The intensive package usually lasts for 48 hours to enable the person to be sustained over the period of crisis. After this period, the co-ordinators review the care package. The original level of support may need to be continued or may be reduced to a maintenance level. REACT is able to stay involved for up to seven days. Following this the service user is transferred to the social services community adult team, if ongoing social care is required. REACT is also able to organise brief respite care for service users who are unable to return home. REACT may be used to complement the role of the hospital social work team. For example, if a patient is suddenly deemed medically ready for discharge and a suitable care package is not in place, REACT can facilitate the discharge by providing the initial care service and straightforward equipment such as walking frames or commodes.

As with Halfway Home, the REACT Project Board met at monthly intervals at first. The Board consisted of senior nurse managers from the hospital trust and community trust and senior social workers. Initially the Board monitored the setting up of the project and later evaluated whether REACT was having any impact on managing winter pressures. This evaluation was very positive. Evidence presented by the REACT co-ordinators to the Project Board demonstrated that the team had made a positive contribution in four areas. First, the team had prevented a significant number of inappropriate admissions to hospital. In the first 15 months, 734 potential admissions were prevented (Burton 2000, p.15). Second, because of REACT's location in the accident and emergency department, the hospital social work team had received fewer duty referrals from this unit. Third, at the beginning of the project, the local social services community adult teams expressed concern about their budgetary constraints, namely, if REACT implemented intensive care packages for clients, reducing these in the future might be problematic. So far, this has not emerged as a problem. Fourth, the establishment of a strong, cohesive multi-agency team has illustrated that collaboration and partnership is possible. Willingness to cross professional boundaries is crucial to the functioning of the team. For example, in the absence of the social worker nurses are able to undertake a social assessment.

Palliative Care Group

The 'Palliative Care Group' is a large multi-disciplinary team. The team's overall aim is to develop palliative services to meet local needs by providing holistic assessments which take into account health, social and spiritual needs. The group discusses individual people and provides information and training for professionals. A significant area where collaborative planning is essential is working with people who have been diagnosed with terminal cancer. When planning for terminal care at home, a combination of care is provided from health and social services resources. Ms B's experience illustrates the benefits of providing a collaborative approach.

MS B

Ms B was 52 years old and had been diagnosed with ovarian and breast cancer and a cerebral secondary cancer. Her prognosis was very poor. Ms B was married and had two children, the younger still living at home. It was Ms B's wish to be cared for at home and her family wanted this to happen. Although supportive of his partner's decision, Mr B stated that he could only accept the role of main carer if he could continue to work part time.

A very complex multi-agency care package was needed to support Ms B and her family. A number of professionals were involved in the planning:

- the Palliative Care Group
- social services home care
- occupational therapists
- a Macmillan nurse
- a hospice at home scheme and a day hospice.

Because of shortage of resources from both social services and health services, initially the care package which was devised left some hours uncovered but, as Ms B's condition deteriorated, the workers involved in the case revised the plan to include a night sitting service and to provide care for one extra afternoon to enable the daughter living at home to have some leisure time. The services provided in relation to Ms B were reviewed by phone on a weekly basis by the workers involved. If one team member considered that the care package needed adjusting, the rest of the group accepted this view. This had positive outcomes for both health and social services and for the recipients of the service.

At a time of limited resources, collaborative working can be difficult to achieve. Resource shortages can mean planners cannot always commit resources. However, as the services provided for Ms B illustrate, closer collaborative planning and partnership mean that a number of different budgets can be accessed.

Conclusion

The four examples of collaboration which have been discussed in this chapter have demonstrated that health and social services can work together towards common goals. Our experience has been that they are able to form good working relationships and have shown a willingness to share scarce resources in order to provide a better service to users. Collaborative work of this kind requires negotiation – and sheer hard work. The following factors seem to be critical to its success:

- Communication: this is so obvious yet its absence, or underestimation, is often the factor which damages the collaborative process.

- Trust: this can only be maintained between individual workers if it is underpinned by support for collaborative working among senior managers. Trust is the basis for building working relationships and respect for each other's roles and professional expertise.

- Resources: in addition to an ongoing sense of resources being scarce, from time to time individual services experience acute financial crises. Collaborative working requires the sharing of scarce resources at such pressure points.

- Joint training: the shared experience brought about by multi-agency training is invaluable in terms of learning about the work of other disciplines.

Our experience of collaborative work has thrown up a couple of constraints. First, separate budgets. Having access to a shared budget would enable workers to access finance and other resources more quickly. Our earlier discussion of the policy background indicated the developments in train in relation to pooling budgets. Second, separate information technology systems. Although we are aware of the need for confidentiality, overlapping roles and responsibilities suggest the need for a shared IT system.

Promoting the factors which lead to benefits from collaboration and working on the constraints is becoming increasingly pressing as central government develops its agenda on strategic planning, service commissioning and service delivery. In addition, there is now, as we have seen, more emphasis on pooling budgets and a strong emphasis on moving from collaboration between health and social services to partnership (Department of Health 1998b). From hospital social workers' perspective, these developments have important implications. Our health colleagues are keen to develop as multi-skilled workers. Already within the hospital in which we work, at least two qualified nurses have undertaken university-based social care courses. Nurses and social workers may be increasingly in competition for the same territory, with nurses moving into counselling, care management and community liaison (McLeod and Bywaters 2000, p.107). Nevertheless, we believe that hospital social work does and will continue to occupy a key profile because of the importance accorded to it by government policies. The core task of hospital social work teams will continue to be planning the discharge of patients. However, we can envisage the emergence of specialist multi-disciplinary teams comprising both health and social services personnel and in such circumstances we would suggest that it is both possible and desirable to move from collaboration to partnership.

Note

1   The term 'guest' is used as the patient has technically been discharged from hospital. As the person has agreed to a stay at Halfway Home 'guest' implies that s/he has made a positive choice and is less formal than 'patient'.

Chapter Five

Working with Health
Partnership in a Community Setting

Barbara Walters

Introduction

This chapter gives an account of five projects, which have been developed by a team providing social services for adults, originally established in preparation for the implementation of the National Health Service and Community Care Act (1990). The team covers a large geographical area, which is mainly rural, but it also serves some larger towns. It is based in three community offices and is responsible for providing services to several small community hospitals. The team's remit is to assess the needs of individuals who have problems caused by disability or mental health problems[1] and to design, provide and review care plans to meet the needs which are identified.

As with other statutory agencies, the team provides services in accordance with strategies emanating from central and local government. These strategies have concentrated increasingly on the need to work in partnership with health colleagues in order to provide preventive and rehabilitative services, aimed at maintaining independence and reducing unnecessary admission to residential care and hospital. In order to secure extra resources for the projects which are described in this chapter, the health and social services had to demonstrate that the extra resources allocated would be ploughed into spending plans jointly owned by health and social services. In addition, the money needed to be used to prevent people entering the care system or hospital and to rehabilitate people already in hospital. The following projects were formulated and agreed by health and social services:

- General Practice-attached social worker
- Community Rehabilitation and Assessment Team for older people
- multi-agency care scheme

- Away to Home scheme
- Partnerships in Action.

The next section provides a brief overview of the legal and policy framework and of the departmental context, which together provided the backdrop to the development of these joint projects. In providing an account of the five initiatives, the chapter demonstrates how ideas about partnership can be translated into practice without formal authority, if workers are willing to co-operate and take risks. In describing the work undertaken, the chapter indicates how achievements can be secured, as well as identifying lessons which can be learned for the development of partnerships in the future.

The policy context

In 1993, Warwickshire Social Services Department reorganised to accommodate the demands of the Children Act (1989) and the National Health Service and Community Care Act (1990). The latter Act transferred responsibility for funding residential and nursing home care from the Department of Social Security to local authorities, with the aim of reducing expenditure (see Chapter One). Local authorities were given the responsibility of assessing people's needs and providing care to meet those needs, with a strong emphasis on maximising independence and rehabilitation. Budgetary constraints meant that priority had to be given to those in greatest need and the expectation was that social services departments would work with health services to provide a 'seamless' service to them. Assessments would be multi-agency and care packages jointly provided, with one person (from one of the agencies) being designated as the care manager. In other words, there was an implied expectation that social workers would work closely with health colleagues to develop a culture of trust in each other's expertise and judgement. The team whose work is the subject of this chapter welcomed opportunities to develop closer working relationships with health colleagues and become involved in joint developments. The projects with which the team became involved anticipated or were influenced by government initiatives which emphasised the theme of partnership.

A number of government reports have been influential in promoting joint initiatives between health and social services (Department of Health 1997a, 1997b, 1998a, 1998b, 1998c, 1999a). For example, the importance of such initiatives was emphasised in *The New National Health Service: Modern, Dependable* (Department of Health 1997b) which identified the development of Health Improvement Programmes (HIMPs) as a key task for health authorities. HIMPs are local strategies for improving health and meeting need in specific localities. Local authorities must be involved in their preparation. Simultaneously, *Better Services for Vulnerable People* (Department of Health 1997a) required all health and local authorities to draw up Joint Investment Plans, by April 1999, for developing services to help people get the care they need, while avoiding unnecessary hospital or care home admissions. This includes the development of specialist rehabilitation services to help people to go home after a hospital stay.

This was followed by *Modernising Social Services* (Department of Health 1998a) which set out three priorities: promoting independence, improving consistency and providing convenient, user-led services. It forewarned of future legislation which would ensure greater integration of care between health and social services and better partnership with housing and other services. The *National Priorities Guidance* (Department of Health 1998d) developed the wider theme of promoting independence as a means of helping people maintain a healthy and active life. It sets out specific joint health and social service goals: to reduce the risk of loss of independence, as a result of unplanned and avoidable admission to hospital; to prevent or delay loss of independence by developing a range of services; and to support carers by the provision of appropriate information. It stresses the importance of taking into account the wider context of housing in drawing up plans. The *National Strategy for Carers* (Department of Health 1999c) made funds available for 'promoting independence' for informal carers. Health Improvement Programmes, Joint Investment Plans and Waiting List Initiatives (a scheme providing resources to reduce the number of those awaiting hospital admission) have all made reference to the need for preventive and rehabilitative approaches. In summary, the following themes have been promoted:

- the prioritisation and development of rehabilitation services to support the independence of older people
- reduction in the risk of unplanned and avoidable admission to hospital and residential care
- provision of information and development of a range of services to support carers
- the establishment of closer working relationships with housing services.

Underpinning these themes is the view that the pattern of provision at that time was distorted as it caused costs to spiral upwards, while not constituting an efficient use of limited resources. In Warwickshire, this view was confirmed by older people themselves, when they were involved in joint reviews of services and joint planning groups looking at rehabilitation for older people.

The government, as well as raising expectations about the service outcomes that health and social services will deliver, also prescribes the process by which those expectations will be achieved, mainly by integrating health and social service planning and service delivery. Accordingly, social services has been a key agency involved in drawing up Joint Investment Plans, creating Health Improvement Plans and agreeing the use of 'Winter Pressures' and 'Waiting List' monies. These monies are 'one-off' grants made by the government to reduce waiting lists for acute hospital beds and to avoid the need for people to remain in hospital when they no longer need to be there. Social services departments are also represented on primary care groups. Primary care groups replaced GP fund-holders and health authorities as purchasers of health care at the local level.

Another key aspect of the process of delivering government expectations concerning service outcomes is the use of performance indicators, such as those established for social services departments by the performance assessment framework stemming from *Modernising Social Services* (Department of Health 1998a). Many of the performance indicators for health have an impact on social services, and vice versa, or rely on joint approaches to a particular issue if the required level of performance is to be reached. As a result, promoting independence and working with the National Health Service are now key objectives for Warwickshire Social Services Department and form part of the County Council's corporate business plan which states, 'We will jointly commit, with the Health Authority, money for new schemes which will enable older people to be supported at home, reducing the likelihood of residential, nursing home or hospital care' (Warwickshire County Council 2000). Similarly, the *Joint Agency Community Care Plan* reports that, 'The lead care agencies are strengthening the development of joint agency planning through developing locality planning/commissioning which will strengthen the integration of health and social services on the ground' (Warwickshire Social Services Department 2000).

A final means by which service outcomes are to be improved is the pooling of budgets. This was signalled in 1998 in *Partnership in Action* (Department of Health 1998b) which reinforced the need for health and social services personnel to work closely together, heralded the intention of the government to put the needs of service users and carers at the forefront of health and social services provision and promised to make working together much easier. This was to be achieved by enabling health and social services budgets to be pooled into a joint budget which could be used to commission and provide services, making it easier for staff to put together comprehensive integrated packages of care. There would be Lead Commissioners from either the health authority, the primary care trust or the social services department who would take responsibility for commissioning both health and social care, on the basis of these functions having been delegated to them by the other partners. This would eliminate overlaps and gaps by integrating the provision of care in ways which allowed health trusts to provide more social services and social services departments to provide a limited range of health services, for example, chiropody and physiotherapy, in contract with the National Health Service. Section 31 of the Health Act (1999) put *Partnership in Action* onto the statute book with the aim of streamlining the provision of services currently provided by a number of agencies.

The NHS Plan (Department of Health 2000a) summarises the goal of all of this policy development in a way which is particularly pertinent to the accounts of the projects which follow: 'In future, the NHS and local Social Services should support older people to make a faster recovery from illness, encouraging independence rather than institutional care and providing reliable, high quality on-going support at home.' (p.125)

Caring for People: Community Care in the Next Decade and Beyond (Griffiths 1988) expected local authorities to work closely with health colleagues but it is only recently that such a requirement has been formalised into a more structured approach, which has replaced more informal developments. As a result, guidelines from within Warwickshire Social Services Department now support the policy and legal frameworks in obliging us to work more closely with colleagues in other services and settings. We decided to use this opportunity in order to examine ways of working more closely with colleagues from health and other agencies.

General practice-attached social worker

Prior to the community care reforms, the team had a social worker linked to a general practice. This was possible because social work teams had small numbers of staff, covered very localised areas and worked with adults and children. As a result, there was the potential for relatively autonomous approaches to the use of the team's resources. Following the reorganisation of social services in response to the National Health Service and Community Care Act (1990) and the Children Act (1989), the teams became larger and were separated into Children's Teams and Adult Teams. The need for consistency across larger geographical areas became a priority. The resultant tighter managerial control over practice led to increasing prioritisation of service users' needs and less flexibility in how resources were allocated. In this more constrained climate, some practice possibilities were closed down, including social workers' involvement with general practice.

However, the need for close working relationships with primary health care staff was confirmed by an audit of our referrals, which showed that the majority of our requests for services came from general practitioners or staff employed in primary health care. The team acknowledged the need for close collaboration with such staff. The case recording system, for example, required the inclusion of input from health professionals in service packages and team members were meeting regularly with district nurses to decide on the content of service packages and the allocation of tasks. This maintained and developed relationships between staff on a day-to-day level but we wanted to examine other ways of working more closely with primary health care staff. However, our resources would not stretch to the allocation of specific social workers to each general practice.

The team was fortunate in having staff who had good working experiences with some of the general practices in the district. In some areas, general practices had a social worker with whom to liaise and who was able to update them on social services developments. One general practitioner had a long history of joint working with social services and, prior to the reorganisation following the community care reforms, had had an informal arrangement whereby a social worker had worked with the patients of the practice. His aim was to continue this and have a social worker who would work solely with his patients, through the maintenance of an active caseload and the provision of a service to any of his patients on request, and who would be engaged with other staff in the practice in developing services for the local community. For example there was a wish to improve the transport services in a very rural community and to develop a bathing service and a housework service for people who were not eligible for help from the statutory services. Furthermore, the general practitioners in this practice are responsible for beds at the local community hospital, which provides care for people discharged from acute hospital who are not fit for discharge home, and an assessment service for other patients. The practice wanted the additional social work help so that there would be an identified social worker for the hospital to ensure that discharges were not delayed and that the communication between social services staff and hospital staff would be more direct.

It was the advent of GP fund-holding, which gave general practitioners the opportunity to hold their own budgets for staffing, drugs and hospital treatment, that finally provided the means to achieve this practice's aspirations for social work input. The practice was able to employ its own social worker. The social services Adult Team entered into a partnership with the practice, which resulted in the practice paying the salary of a half-time social worker and the social services department paying for the social worker's travel expenses, office accommodation, equipment and supervision. It was of mutual benefit to have a social worker who could develop close links with the local community hospital to ensure that throughput of patients was maintained. The general practitioner was happy to have an identified social worker who would establish contact with all hospital patients at an early stage, whether or not they were eligible for social services help, in order to assist with any issues which might delay discharge and to provide any information needed to facilitate services. The general practitioner achieved his aim of having a social worker involved in working with other members of his team and we were reassured that his team would not try to include the wider social work team in any community developmental work as we do not have enough social workers to develop non-essential services.

This practice has a general practitioner who is very supportive of social services and he had some difficulty in understanding why we could not be involved in all of the activities of the practice staff as many activities were specifically medical. It was acknowledged that if he appointed his own social worker he would have some choice in the activities of that worker. We developed a shared philosophy of planning and developing services to meet needs and working with local people to promote a healthier community. When fund-holding GP practices were replaced by primary care groups, the local primary care group decided to continue to fund this post as it has become more focused on hospital discharge and there is increasing pressure to ensure that patients do not stay in hospital longer than they need to. The creation of the post has enabled an ongoing dialogue between social services and hospital staff which has resulted in a shared understanding of problems and more joint solutions to them. Pressure on hospital beds and the need to provide services which meet government targets have focused activity on essentials so that the time available for developing non-priority services is reduced for everyone. However, the fact that the post is targeted on hospital discharge increases the possibility of further such posts being funded by the primary care group.

Community Rehabilitation and Assessment Team for older people

This scheme anticipated the proposals in *Modernising Social Services* (Department of Health 1998a), which required services to be provided which promoted independence, reduced the loss of independence after an unplanned and avoidable admission to hospital and aimed to prevent such admissions to hospital. The health authority declared its intention to pilot a Community Rehabilitation and Assessment Team for older people. The scheme brought together the work of the local authority's strategy committee on the future direction of care for older people and the existing joint agreement between health and social services in relation to continuing health care. The vision of future services was that they would: provide care closer to people's homes; prevent unneccesary hospital admission; and introduce preventive services to people much sooner than was then the normal practice. It was also intended that rehabilitation should be proactive, which meant it would be available to people in their homes rather than simply as a reaction to a hospital stay. The decision was made to pilot a scheme to compensate for a recent reduction in the number of beds at the local hospital in the main town in the centre of the district. The services at the local hospital had gradually declined over a number of years and, for some time, had consisted of two wards for older people. One of these wards then closed, which left just one ward, with beds managed by local general practitioners. The closure of this ward had created a public outcry as well as putting pressure on the nearby acute hospitals, as patients could not be transferred from those hospitals to the local hospital in order to release acute beds.

A steering group was formed, consisting of representatives of the community trust, the general practitioners who managed the beds at the hospital, the health authority and social services. Subsequently, a multi-disciplinary team was created consisting of community nurses (one of whom is the co-ordinator), health care assistants, social worker, speech and language therapist, physiotherapist and occupational therapist. The team provides a seven-day-a-week service. Referrals are received from general practitioners, social workers or community nurses acting on behalf of service users. The co-ordinator receives all referrals and decides who else needs to be involved in the care plan. Care under the scheme is provided for one month and can be provided by health care assistants or local authority home helps or a combination of both.

The scheme had to overcome a number of difficulties in the early stages of its planning. First, the pilot scheme had difficulty finding care staff in an area where the employment opportunities are many and varied and it also took some time to recruit the health care assistants. Second, social services could not provide staffing resources and so the health authority financed a social worker, occupational therapist and weekend home care supervisor. Third, district nurses initially did not welcome the scheme, as the work required was in addition to their normal workload. To overcome this difficulty extra staff were recruited. Fourth, an additional complication at the start of the scheme arose in relation to service charges. Social services charge people for using their services but the health authority does not. Social services agreed to waive charges for people receiving care under the scheme. Fifth, a good deal of time had to be spent encouraging doctors to use the scheme. Initially general practitioners forgot about the scheme or were sceptical about the services it could provide. They were also frustrated at the amount of time it took to make a referral before the co-ordinator, who now receives all referrals, was appointed. Sixth, retraining was necessary for the home care staff. Traditionally home care is used to 'do things' for people and the workers on this scheme had to encourage people to learn to do things themselves.

Once these difficulties were overcome, the response provided by the team proved to be rapid and comprehensive. Assessments are undertaken within three hours of initial referrals. The co-ordinator then initiates a multi-disciplinary approach to care, which can include night-sits. People have the choice between receiving services from the team or being admitted to hospital. Referral evidence suggests that the people who have benefited most from the service are those who have chest or urinary infections, who have suffered mild strokes or whose carers have been admitted to hospital. Few of the users would have been eligible for services from the social services department if they had not been on the scheme, as they did not meet the department's priority criteria. The department's services are targeted on those in greatest need and those who are not eligible for our services are usually given information about where the help they need might be available.

An evaluation of the work of the Community Rehabilitation and Assessment Team by the community trust regarded it as successful. It has improved inter-agency working and blurred traditional professional roles and boundaries. Through multi-agency working, assessments are not duplicated, although the scheme has yet to develop an assessment format which suits everyone. The cost of care under the scheme is less than the cost of in-patient care and the majority of the people referred to the scheme have maintained or improved their independence as a result of the intervention of the Community Rehabilitation and Assessment Team.

Multi-agency care scheme

The multi-agency care scheme, in the west of the district, was a joint project facilitated by health and social services and an independent provider. The aims of the project were to: improve the rehabilitation of older people; prevent unnecessary admission to hospital; provide health and social services residential care within the local community and in a homely environment.

The scheme involved services provided by an old Victorian hospital. The two traditional 'Florence Nightingale' wards provided twenty-two beds. The other facility under review was a residential care home for older people with twenty-one beds, of which the local authority purchased use of fifteen. Originally the residential home was owned by the local authority, which made an attempt to close it, as the standard of the building was unacceptable. The local residents, who saw it as a resource for the community, successfully opposed closure. The management of the residential home was transferred from the local authority to a voluntary organisation.

The social services department, the health authority, the voluntary organisation and the health care NHS trust formed a partnership to develop a comprehensive range of health and social services. By pooling the combined local resources of the four organisations they sought to reconfigure services on one site to reflect local need. In order to progress this project a steering group was formed, consisting of the chief officers of the four organisations, and a project group was established, with members from the commissioning and operational staff. The steering group decided that the local community should be involved in the decision-making process about what services were needed and how they should be provided. A whole-day conference was arranged to enable this to be done and the ideas and concerns expressed at the conference were incorporated into the plans.

The local community made a number of requests. First, that the residential home and the hospital should remain to provide residential care and nursing home care. Second, that a centre should be available from which voluntary and statutory agencies could provide information for patients and carers on a variety of subjects in health promotion services. Third, because of lack of public transport, that the site should accommodate an out-patient clinic to which people could go for treatment. Fourth, that social services home care should be on the same site as district nursing, with easier access to equipment to facilitate rehabilitation and independence.

In order to make progress, the project group had to take on board the key points raised at the conference by the local community, but also had to consider the wider strategic policy, and the financial constraints, of the health authority and social services department. In considering possible tensions between community and organisational concerns, a number of issues had to be borne in mind. The local community had expressed a need for residential facilities at both the residential home and the hospital, but there had to be economies of scale to ensure that the residential development was financially viable for the voluntary organisation. Nursing and residential care beds had to be serviced at minimum cost which meant that an appropriate skill mix of staff had to be recruited. The local community was concerned about excessive development on the site and needed reassurance that services would be reconfigured, not reduced.

The steering group put the following proposals to the local community. First, that they would recruit a Community Rehabilitation and Assessment Team. This team would be developed along the same lines as the team discussed in the previous section, which had been judged to be a success. The Community Rehabilitation and Assessment Team would have access to the facilities on the site.

Second, that a sixty-bed residential facility would be provided. The residential establishment would be divided into smaller units, with the intention that staff could be shared across the units to ensure adequate staffing. The residential facility would have twelve health care beds, funded by the health authority, which would provide rehabilitation for those discharged from the acute hospitals in the area and provide respite support to families coping with chronic illness. Access to these beds would be via the local general practitioners. Thirteen nursing home beds would be available; the local authority would purchase four of these for people needing long-term nursing home care. One of the units would provide residential care. It was anticipated that social services would purchase seven of the beds for respite and long-term care, with the remainder being allocated by the voluntary organisation. Another unit would provide residential care for older people with mental ill health.

Third, that a day centre would be provided. The day centre would be open seven days a week providing social day care and therapeutic day care for local people. The site would also be used for day care for older people who were mentally confused. Fourth, that an Information and Advice Centre would offer a range of information to the local community. The Centre would be used by voluntary agencies on a sessional basis to provide the information and advice. Fifth, that one of the local general practices would be relocated to the site, so that the services of a general practitioner and district nurses would be available. Finally, it was the steering group's intention to provide a broader range of out-patient clinics at the new local hospital site for various services.

This was an ambitious scheme requiring merging of services, roles and responsibilities. The extent of this was only realised as the project progressed and it became impossible to resolve the problem of clinical accountability in the event of any untoward incident. This scheme is, therefore, in abeyance pending resolution of that problem.

Away to Home Scheme

Each district of the social services department has a multi-disciplinary panel to discuss and advise on eligibility for residential and nursing home care. The panels have representatives from acute hospital and community trusts as well as social services and the health authority. Our panel also includes a housing association which purchased the stock of public housing from the district council. The inclusion of a housing association representative meant that the panel had the possibility of recommending that people should try sheltered housing, rather than residential care, because those people who had been considered by the panel were regarded as in greatest need and attracted maximum points on the housing waiting list. This led to a decision that we should have a discrete scheme, which would delay or prevent the admission of people to residential care. The social services manager, who chairs this panel, had previously managed a residential care home and was committed to ensuring that only those people who could not be maintained at home were admitted to residential care. This fitted with the criteria, agreed by the health authority and social services, which people had to meet in order to be considered eligible for public funding for residential care. Initially the scheme was funded by money given by the government to ease anticipated pressures in acute hospitals during the winter, but this was insufficient and there were problems in securing sufficient funding for the project to proceed. Additional funding became available as the scheme began to fit with the government's priorities for rehabilitation.

There are three parts to the scheme. The first component consists of three flats which were made available by the housing association in different areas of the locality and are rented to the scheme. These were furnished and are two-bedroom flats with shared kitchens and bathrooms. Staff were recruited who have rehabilitation as the focus of their work. This part of the scheme is intended to benefit:

- People who are presented to the panel, but who are on the fringe of eligibility for residential care. They are referred to the scheme for an assessment of their ability and potential for rehabilitation in a homely setting.

- People judged to have completed their medical episode in hospital, but who are referred for residential care, can spend time in the flats so that an assessment can be made of their potential for improvement.

- People who are referred for residential care but who wish to remain in their own home can have time for assessment and rehabilitation to help them decide on their future.

- Those whose main carer has been admitted to hospital or has died or who wish to separate from their carer can be admitted to the scheme, rather than hospital or residential care, so that an assessment can be made of their abilities and they can be helped to greater independence.

The second part of the scheme is designed to enable tenants in very sheltered housing complexes to remain there. Many of the tenants who transfer to residential care are cared for to a significant extent by their partners in the residential care home. We decided, therefore, to develop the care in very sheltered housing schemes so that tenants can remain and carers can have support to enable them to care for their partners in their own homes. The rehabilitation workers are available to provide additional care as well as that provided by the more traditional home care service.

The third part of the scheme is designed to enrich the lives of the tenants in the three sheltered schemes in which the flats are located. We provide funds to Age Concern to enable them to offer a befriending service for tenants and their carers, an advice service and a range of social activities, in conjunction with the wardens of the complexes, so that carers can have a social life without worrying about the person for whom they care. We are also working with the housing association to provide a shopping and housework service to people in sheltered housing schemes who do not meet the department's criteria for the provision of services.

Two factors have been identified as critical to the success of the Away to Home scheme. First, there has to be dedicated occupational therapy input and a co-ordinator to ensure that reviews are held and plans are made which are consistent with the objectives of the scheme. Second, it has been important to have a meeting which includes everyone who has been involved in the care of the prospective user of the service, so that all understand the rationale and the objectives and are committed to its success.

It was anticipated that all agencies working with prospective users would welcome the scheme. However, as with some of those involved in the Community Rehabilitation and Assessment Team, not everyone could co-operate at first. Hospitals were anxious about putting people, who they believed needed residential care, 'at risk' by keeping them in the community without 24-hour care. Wardens felt threatened by the activities planned by Age Concern and fearful that they would have to provide care for more vulnerable people. Social workers were torn by their need to advocate for service users and their relatives and the social services department's requirements to try to maintain people at home. The scheme also seemed to conflict with the department's guidance on the amount of home care available to individuals. It took longer than anticipated to recruit rehabilitation staff and we had to await the completion of alterations to the housing accommodation before we could proceed. We came to realise how important it was to try to understand these different agendas and anticipate them in the planning process.

We are now beginning to see the benefits of the scheme. Four people who were referred for residential care are now living in their own very sheltered flats. Two people who were already living in one of the housing complexes have been helped to remain there. One person who is currently in residential care would like to move to his own accommodation and he will join the scheme to assess his potential for this. As professionals have seen the success of the scheme they have become more enthusiastic about referring people who might benefit from it.

Partnerships in Action

The last project to be discussed is Partnerships in Action, which was a response to the Department of Health paper (1998b) of a similar name. The project was initiated by a group of people who were keen to develop a more effective relationship between the local community health trust and the primary care group. The chief executive of the community trust wrote a paper, which was agreed by the trust board, outlining how the trust could work more effectively with the primary care group. The locality for the pilot project was chosen for a number of reasons.

First, there was an excellent relationship between the staff of the community trust and the local general practitioners. Second, there was an established philosophy of investment in community services and the community hospital in providing services for the local community. Third, good relationships existed between social services and general practices. (One of the practices involved is the practice employing its own social worker – see section beginning on p.88). Fourth, the social services, district nursing, and general practice teams in this locality had a reputation for being forward thinking and innovative. All these factors were considered to be important to the success of the scheme.

The planning group appointed a co-ordinator, who was responsible for the management and co-ordination of the community hospital, community nursing staff and the local staff in professions allied to medicine. The original plan was that the co-ordinator would have staffing and non-staffing budgets and would have discussions with social services to see whether local team budgets could be included. In practice this was not viable. Budgets became a secondary consideration as all professionals committed themselves to working on proposals for improving services and developing working relationships with health colleagues.

A locality project group was formed with membership from the three general practices, including the general practitioners, practice staff from the community trust, district nurses and health visitors. Members were also recruited from the community hospital, primary care group, voluntary sector and social services. The locality project group decided on six areas of work. Six groups were formed. The facilitators of the groups were members of the project group and co-opted other members as needed. The six areas of work were:

The prevention of coronary heart disease and the rehabilitation of people who have this disease

The project group worked up a list of protocols. As a result of the project, a physiotherapist has been appointed and exercise equipment has been purchased. The group will be recruiting volunteers to organise walks for people in the community.

Mental health services

The aim was to clarify the referral process and the role of professionals involved. This group was short-lived as major changes were being planned and introduced, following the specific requirements laid down in *Modernising Mental Health* (Department of Health 2000b).

Care of older people

The group discussed a definition of 'old age'. Concern was expressed that people between the ages of 65 and 75 were likely to be increasingly ignored, as few agencies target their services at this age group. Limited resources and financial constraints often prevented agencies from offering services to any but the older people with high levels of need. The decision was that this group should aim at prevention of illness. It was agreed that all practices would offer health screening to people of this age group who would then be given a folder of information detailing the services which would be available, if and when they were needed, and promoting healthy lifestyles.

People who had strokes

One of the practices in the locality already had a stroke protocol, which had been developed in line with government objectives and health authority protocols. The protocol advocates multi-disciplinary rehabilitation and appropriate follow-up after hospital discharge. There is an emphasis on the prevention of future strokes and ultimate independence.

Patient-held records

The group tried to develop a single multi-disciplinary patient-held record for use by all health and social services personnel. It was hoped that this would be computerised so that it would be accessible to all the agencies involved in someone's care. The purpose was to avoid duplication, provide useful information for service users and improve communication between professionals. It was anticipated that the record would enable the level and quality of care to be measured. Unfortunately, because of health confidentiality procedures, this goal has had to be limited to the sharing of paper records, which are left with the service user, between health staff. There seems little possibility of sharing computer records in the near future.

Multi-disciplinary teamwork

The group worked towards developing flexible ways of sharing resources, including staff time. The aim was to develop a holistic way of working, while recognising the unique contribution of each profession. Protocols would be developed and training provided. The group has already achieved some of its aims, by providing joint training for health and social services staff on moving and handling people. This joint training has benefited service users, as the techniques used for handling are now the same for all staff working in our residential care homes, home care, the hospital and district nurses. It has also resulted in more sharing of care between social services and health staff. District nurses are now training staff in the local authority residential care home to do simple dressings and administer insulin. This reduces the impact of frequent 'comings and goings' on the frail residents of the home.

Partnerships in Action has been a success. Membership of the groups has been flexible in order to allow people with specific types of expertise to be co-opted. Success has been achieved despite the fact that the initiative began at a time of financial restraint for social services and the health authority and with each authority having different eligibility criteria for access to services. The transfer of care from health professionals to social services has raised questions about budgetary issues, which will always be present when financial resources are scarce and competition for them is great. Despite these constraints the projects have fulfilled their aims.

Wider implications

These five projects all set out with high hopes and great enthusiasm to find ways of health, social services and other agencies working together. All agencies had limited finances and wanted to find ways of avoiding duplication and maximising the resources available. All were aimed at preventing unnecessary hospital admission and facilitating early discharge. All were focused on preventing admission to residential care and on maintaining people in their own homes. Several lessons have been learned from these projects.

First, that it is possible to effect change if there is goodwill and the determination to do so. Legislation and regulation are not needed. They are helpful if money is needed, however! Second, it is important not to be too carried away by enthusiasm for a project. Others, whose co-operation is vital, may have reservations and these need to be heard and resolved. Third, however much we are required by legislation and regulation to work together there remains a problem caused by our different professional ethics, particularly in relation to the extent to which people should be able to put themselves at risk. As was outlined above, this emerged as an issue in Away to Home with hospital staff wanting people to go into residential care to be 'safe', rather than experience the risks of living in their own home, with which social workers are more comfortable.

Fourth, problems are caused by detail. Although we are required to work together and pool budgets, sorting out some of the detail about how this is to be achieved is difficult. The multi-agency care scheme is stuck because there is no acceptable solution to the problem of legal liability in the event of an 'untoward incident'. The Partnerships in Action project has overcome the problems of professional accountability but the allegiance people have to members of the same profession, together with awareness of budget pressures, hampers the formation of new relationships in both health and social services. Fifth, it is difficult to pool budgets when money is committed to existing users and services. Finally, joint assessments and shared records cannot reach their full potential as long as current restrictions on the sharing of information are in existence.

Note

1   The team assesses adults, of whatever age, who have needs due to physical disabilities, learning disabilities or mental health problems. ('Age' does not appear in this connection in Warwickshire Social Services Department, because growing older is not regarded as a problem in itself.)

Chapter Six

Empowerment as a Participative Process

Linda Fleming and Carole McSparran

Introduction

The concept of empowerment underpinned the legislation which led to the implementation of the community care reforms (Stevenson and Parsloe 1993, p.9), following the Griffiths Report (1988). It was placed centre-stage in the influential Managers' and Practitioners' Guides to Care Management and Assessment (Social Services Inspectorate 1991a, 1991b), which gave the empowerment of service users and carers as the overarching rationale for the reforms. The word 'empowerment' has cropped up with increasing frequency in the field of community care ever since and it has remained a fashionable term in debates about the direction in which community care practice should develop. It has had a considerable impact on social work (Dalrymple and Burke 1995, p.48) and has been promoted as signifying a redistribution of power from workers to users so that the latter are enabled to gain more control over their lives. In what is by now a well-established mixed economy of care, empowerment is based on assumptions that social work relates to service users in their status as consumers, with rights to minimum standards of service and choice (Barnes and Wistow 1994).

The emphasis on empowerment has been criticised at times as being idealistic and at other times as tokenistic, given that financial controls on budgets restrict services, with warnings that it can be reduced to a mere buzz-word (Mullender and Ward 1991; Braye and Preston-Shoot 1995). There is plenty of scope for a mismatch between evoking the image of a consumer, with money to spend, and the reality of users of social services, who do not have the financial resources to use the 'care market' as they might choose. In the context of limited resources, social workers are engaged in targeting, rationing and making budget-led decisions: activities which sit uneasily with the notion of empowering service users.

This chapter describes a team's attempt to consider the rhetoric of empowerment against the reality of its practice. In so doing, the team brought together the 'high ground' of theory on empowerment and 'the swampy lowlands' of day-to-day practice (Schön 1992, in Thompson 2000, p.41).

A study reflecting on practice

For busy practitioners in statutory social work it is all too easy to become focused on carrying out assessments and providing services simply as a set of 'procedures', without considering the content of the intervention. In our team[1], we aim to raise awareness regularly about the nature of our social work practice, in part to guard against perpetuating the oppression of disabled and older people. Following training sessions on anti-oppressive practice, the team decided to examine its practice with service users and carers, using empowerment as a focus. As Thompson (1993, in Adams 1996, p.5) states, empowerment has the potential to combat the multiple oppressions faced by service users. The role social workers play in the empowering process is crucial in determining whether oppression is increased or challenged.

We decided to undertake a small-scale study to ascertain whether service users and carers perceived their receipt of social work and occupational therapy services as empowering. In undertaking the study, we were conscious that 'the empowerment process does not occur in an ordered step-by-step way. It is an ongoing process with shifting goals' (Dalrymple and Burke 1995, p.55). This suggests that empowerment cannot be reduced to a simplistic act, involving an instant transfer of power, but involves working through a *process* of attempting to reduce the powerlessness which service users experience. The study drew on the three levels in Dalrymple and Burke's model of empowerment as a framework for approaching this process (Dalrymple and Burke 1995, pp.53–55). The first level is concerned with the personal experiences of the person feeling powerless – the study listened to and recorded service users' experiences. The second level is the ability to produce and regulate events in one's life – the study indicates the extent to which service users felt they were able to do this. The third level is action – the final part of the chapter considers action taken to establish a service for people 'not eligible' for social services provision.

We decided on the following question for our study: 'Are social work and occupational therapy seen as empowering by service users and carers?' We decided to use semi-structured interviews in which the areas to be covered were predetermined by a questionnaire, in preference to more lengthy unstructured interviews. This approach seemed preferable to sending a list of questions by post, which would have reduced the exploration of issues and would have been impersonal. The questionnaire was based around four dimensions that are identified by Beresford and Croft (1993) as being significant in developing practice which is empowering: first, challenging oppression and discrimination; second, enabling service users to define their own needs; third, providing service users with information and space to be able to have a say in planning and decision-making; finally, equipping people to take power by gaining in confidence and self-esteem. Although not all of the dimensions in Beresford and Croft's typology can be directly applied to the study, we consciously used the four dimensions when constructing the questionnaire and adapted their ideas to a social services department. We discovered that the four dimensions were only realised in the setting up of Direct Payments and in the eventual establishment of the befriending service (discussed later in the chapter). Both of these initiatives involved action (Dalrymple and Burke 1995, p.55).

The potential participants in the study were identified by social workers and occupational therapists in the team and were selected on the basis that staff considered their work with them to be examples of 'good practice'. Fifty service users were identified. Given the time constraints this number was reduced to a more manageable sixteen. The sixteen service users were selected on the basis that the people to be interviewed had to be mentally alert and had to reflect different areas of need. The sample included two men and fourteen women from different economic backgrounds. A third of the participants were under sixty-five years of age, with different physical impairments. Although no carers were interviewed, some service users chose to invite a carer or family member along to the interview. We chose not to interview service users with learning difficulties or severe mental health problems, as the format of the questionnaire did not facilitate their participation. Interviews with Black service users were not possible at the time of our study.[2]

The sixteen potential participants were contacted and asked if they wished to be involved. Eleven of them agreed to be interviewed.[3] All of the interviews took place in the participants' homes. Team members, plus two students on placement, interviewed and completed questionnaires on participants who were previously unknown to them, as this was thought to be a way of distancing the study, to some extent, from participants' routine contact with the social services department. Interviewers stressed that the questionnaires were being used as a vehicle for participants' accounts of their experiences of social workers' and occupational therapists' contact with them. All service users were assured of anonymity when the findings were written up.

Findings from the study

As previously stated, our intention was to ascertain whether social work and occupational therapy services were perceived as empowering by service users and carers. At the level of feelings (Level One in Dalrymple and Burke's model, see above), we concentrated on the interaction with the worker, the contextual aspect (history of events) and the biographical characteristics of the person(s). Dalrymple and Burke see these elements as lying at the core of empowerment (Dalrymple and Burke 1995, p.53). Service users were asked to comment on the social worker or occupational therapist's contact with them and on how they had felt as a result of their involvement in the assessment process. Level Two (in Dalrymple and Burke's model) is the 'level of ideas'. In relation to this level, the study was concerned with examining whether social workers and occupational therapists encouraged and developed service users' and carers' capacity to gain control and achieve change. This would be indicated by service users and carers having access to information, being offered choices and being consulted and involved in the assessment and planning process. The participants' responses were categorised under the following themes: defining the problem; accessibility of information; choice and control; consultation.

DEFINING THE PROBLEM

Under the National Health Service and Community Care Act (1990), social workers have a duty to undertake comprehensive and multi-disciplinary assessments to identify areas of need. Although users and carers are involved in the assessment process, misjudgements can be made by professionals about what is considered to be a priority. The participants in the study suggested that social workers and occupational therapists sometimes underemphasised or overemphasised their problems:

> What happened to me was more of a life-shattering event than a problem. (A)

> In the early months of my rehabilitation, I hardly knew the questions, let alone the answers! As the months rolled on it became easier to understand one's own needs. (J)

Sometimes service users and carers, although aware of their needs, sought assistance from a social worker or occupational therapist in exploring their situation:

[As a result of] trauma injury…you need someone to put it in perspective, to prioritise your needs and to counsel you…for the social worker to be aware of the overall home situation and what might need attention. (J)

ACCESSIBILITY OF INFORMATION

Croft and Beresford state that 'information is power and needs to be shared' (quoted in Dalrymple and Burke 1995, p.137). Information needs to be relevant, clear and readily available. Information should be appropriate to people's abilities, taking into account experience, language, culture, knowledge and disabilities.

The participants were asked whether they understood what could be provided by social services. The responses received demonstrated that the service users did not fully understand the remit of social services. A quarter of the participants interviewed confused social services with social security. This was a surprising result given that some of the participants had been in receipt of services for some considerable time.

Didn't know what to expect…had had no prior contact with social services and only knew they helped people. (D)

Not totally sure, having never come across social services, but the title suggested answers to some of my needs, vague idea but nothing definite. (J)

Information on finance for when a placement in a home may be required. (E)

Information was mediocre really, though in social services' defence, twenty-four years ago there seemed few life options. An early outline of options and possible strategies which hopefully being feasible might have equipped me with the necessary information to make informed choices. I might have done things rather differently. (J)

'J' went on to say that information on services is now available, but it is interesting to note that he listed sources outside of social services:

Nowadays, more accessible information is available such as charities lists, so there is more public awareness as information is shared. A climate of shared information. Information is now much more freely available such as information about Direct Payments and the Complaints Procedure. More information on rights and the impact of legislation is needed though. The Spinal Injury Association started in 1974 and is a very powerful movement. Magazines and the media through all avenues are breaking down the taboos. All this has an impact on social services. (J)

Only half of the respondents felt that the allocated worker was able to facilitate services to provide practical help and none of the respondents felt that the worker could provide advice in obtaining help from other agencies, for example, health, housing and the voluntary sector:

> Family sorted everything. No understanding of services available. (F)

> Social worker advised me on the options open to me with Direct Payments, time required and analysing requirements. (C)

CHOICE AND CONTROL

Empowering practice involves service users having choice and control over the services provided. One aspect of this which emerged from the study concerned service users and carers having some choice about who carried out the assessment. One social worker reported that Mr and Mrs A would have liked an older social worker:

> Mr and Mrs A were emphatic that all of the social workers who had visited them were much younger than themselves. This had been disempowering, in that they did not feel able to share problems with someone younger. They would have preferred to discuss issues with someone older.

In practice, it may be unrealistic to offer a choice of worker. A number of factors need to be taken into account, for example workloads and the make-up of the team. In this Adult Team social workers are attached to general practices, which results in workers dealing with all cases generated from a particular geographical area. Current staffing levels do not allow for the degree of flexibility requested by service users.

Generally service users did not feel in control of the situation nor did they consider that they had been offered any 'real' choice over who was providing the care:

> Mr and Mrs S felt that their life situation left them with no choice or control. The social worker did what was needed but they felt there was only one option anyway.

> Not much choice of carers. (B)

As the next quote illustrates, the environment may also be an obstacle in facilitating discussions with service users about service provision.

> I seemed to have many general conversations skirting big issues with lots of awkward pauses. I was still hospitalised at the time of my first contact and it did not help as hospitals, though a safe environment, are not ideally suited

to deep meaningful conversations about how one is going to survive the future. (J)

CONSULTATION

Participants were asked, 'What could social services have done better for you?' In retrospect it is apparent that this question assumed that people were sufficiently informed about social services to comment and this appeared not to be the case, as we saw earlier. Nevertheless, the findings produced responses which were positive:

Not really able to comment except that I was very happy with the services provided. (D)

They were as helpful as they could be within the constraints of their job. (G)

Provided written information on Direct Payments as promised. (K)

Very supportive and always available. (C)

Other responses were more critical:

More financial assistance would have helped. (A)

Time could have been quicker. Things could have been sorted out more quickly. (E)

Implications of the study

Having deliberately identified potential participants on the basis that they would provide illustrations of good practice in community care, we had anticipated responses from them which would be indicative of a process of empowerment. Instead, the responses received were varied, with service users and carers at times not feeling empowered by social work and occupational therapy services. The study highlighted four important issues for practice.

First, the provision of information appears to be a key factor. Certain written information was thought to be empowering in working with social services, particularly the provision for service users of copies of assessments and care plans, information on the complaints process, the team plan, data protection and access to records. This highlighted the need for widespread publicity explaining the role of a social worker, how to access equipment, how to access the benefits system, the role of Citizens Advice Bureaux, and how to obtain an advocate.

Since the study took place, the availability and distribution of information by the department has improved. For the adult team the study reinforced the need to provide service users with accessible and jargon-free information. It is now standard practice to provide service users with an information pack, describing: the work of the team, the needs and priority levels for service provision (to enable people to decide for themselves whether they are eligible for our services), the comments, complaints and compliments procedures, access to records, charging for services procedures and the out-of-hours service. There are guidance notes on Direct Payments which can be given to service users. As a consequence of this study, the team is currently developing a leaflet describing the roles of the social worker and the occupational therapist.

Second, social workers and occupational therapists should be prepared to 'loosen control and embrace users' own definitions and solutions' (Barnes and Walker 1998, p.202) (See also Richards 2000; Smale, Tuson and Statham 2000). A focus on strict predetermined criteria runs the risk of social workers and occupational therapists defining the problems people have and deciding on the type of work they will do with them. It is important for social workers and occupational therapists to listen to service users' narratives. Listening to someone's story can assist that person to become more confident. This in itself can be empowering.

Third, limited resources have led local authorities to target those people seen to be at greatest risk of losing independence. The end result is social workers calculating priorities based on priority levels and redirecting work that does not meet the criteria. This is done in conjunction with the service users, to enable a shared understanding.

Fourth, although we have listened to the comments from service users about the lack of choice of services and carers in the district, it is unlikely that policies in this area will change. Social workers advocate as far as it is possible, but there are financial restrictions. This is the consequence of several factors: restrictions in the home care agencies that we can use; lack of public transport; the distances to be covered by home carers and costs involved; the unavailability of local carers in a large rural area; increasing requests for home care as a result of speedier hospital discharges.

A befriending service

One of the aims of the study was to look at ways of producing change in the services provided: the third level in Dalrymple and Burke's model, the level of action. One of the issues that emerged from the interviews and questionnaires was the number of older people who were unable to access services because they were assessed as low priority. These people did not meet the criteria for services, in that they only met Level Three of the social services department's 'Needs and Priority Levels' (leaflet number SS.284 (7.95)):

> People in this category have significant levels of need and have third priority call upon our resources. They will only receive help after all people at Levels One and Two have received adequate service. To be in this category both the following criteria must apply: the person has significant difficulty in carrying out essential life tasks and limited assistance is required to constitute a modest care support network or provide limited propping up to an existing one. The assessment of people who appear likely to fall into this category will be carried out within one month in normal circumstances.

As a consequence of the findings from the study, the team began to collate information on all referrals that were identified as low priority, over a six-month period. By the end of the period, referrals were held on 27 older people. The referrals received by social workers reflected the different needs of older people living in the locality. Many of them were lonely and depressed following the death of a partner or discharge from hospital. Others were living in isolated areas with little or no contact with relatives or neighbours. Some older people wanted someone to accompany them to local clubs, to help with shopping, to go with them on walks or to help with the garden.

A report on these findings was submitted to managers. The report requested the setting up of a befriending service using money from a 'low priority budget' to fund it. It was proposed that there would be no charge for the befriending service, as older people assessed as Level Three priority are not eligible to claim Attendance Allowance or Disability Living Allowance. Further discussions about the proposed scheme resulted in the befriending service being provided by Age Concern, and funded by social services, to older people living at home. The befriending service would provide companionship for lonely and isolated people who were not eligible to receive help from social services. Befrienders would also be asked to provide assistance with practical tasks.

A number of planning meetings were held with the proposed manager of the planned befriending service. Age Concern advertised for volunteers in the surrounding areas using the local press and libraries. The manager of the project also spoke to community groups about the scheme. A number of people were recruited and trained as volunteers before the befriending service began. Volunteers have offered assistance in a variety of areas: support and help with issues surrounding grief and loss; outings; companionship; help in the garden; outings to visit relatives and friends; shopping;

walks in the garden and surrounding area; introduction to other support networks. The service has contributed to the alleviation of many of the problems of loneliness and isolation faced by older people in the locality. The users of the befriending service appear to gain a sense of self-worth from being cared about, rather than solely being cared for. Older people have been reconnected with their local community as they have regained confidence in social settings which had become daunting. Part of the success of the service is due to the fact that users of the service define their own needs, and decide on their priorities and preferences. The service provides an ethos in which people achieve their own solutions and we strive to ensure that the service fits the individual's unique range of needs.

In retrospect, we have questioned our initiation of a service based solely on the evidence of our monitoring of referrals. This approach was lacking in consultation and partnership with representative groups of disabled and older people. However, partnership has been repeatedly in evidence with Age Concern, with funding from the department being given directly to Age Concern on an annual basis for the provision of this service. To embody a truly empowering approach we feel that involvement by representative groups (via, for example, Age Concern, carers' groups and the Alzheimer's Disease Society) would have been required at the time of our initial study to confirm or dispute our assumptions.

Conclusion

Two important issues have arisen for the team from the small-scale study of whether service users were empowered. First, the need to consider the power and role of the social worker in the empowerment process and second, confirmation that empowerment is a political process.

In retrospect, the power of social workers is reflected in the fact that the framework for the questionnaire used in our small-scale study partially embodied a 'questioning model' of assessment. In the questioning model of assessment, 'the questions reflect the worker's agenda, not other people's. Embodied in the questions are implicit or explicit perceptions about the problems services users have and preconceptions about the resources available to meet them' (Smale, Tuson and Statham 2000, p.133). This method of information gathering may have advantages in framing information and determining eligibility (which can be useful in measuring physical ability to assist rehabilitation), but the model does not address the fundamental goals of maintaining independence, maximising people's potential and empowering people to exercise choice (Beresford and Croft 1993; Beresford and Turner 1997; Department of Health 1989). Although the framework for the questionnaire was based on the 'questioning model', the practitioners taking part in the study used an 'exchange model' approach when interviewing service users. This is illustrated by practitioners obtaining information that went beyond facts to concentrate on service users' feelings. By using an 'exchange model', the practitioners were able to arrive at a mutual understanding of the service users' concerns or problems and, as a result, to identify services that would be beneficial to people in the district. This is illustrated by the development of the befriending service.

The second important issue we have faced is that our small-scale study confirmed the view that empowering practice is inherently a political activity (Adams 1996). Empowerment is only effective when practitioners are highly motivated to take into account the discrimination and oppression experienced by service users: 'Empowerment is more than a traditional notion of "enabling". It is geared towards helping to equip people for the challenges of tackling the social disadvantages and inequalities they face. Empowerment is not only a psychological process but also a social and political one' (Thompson 2000, p.120). In the light of such definitions of empowerment, it would be easy to view our efforts towards empowering practice as ineffective and tokenistic, but this would devalue our attempts to build on our experiences. The small-scale study undertaken by the team has encouraged practitioners to undertake further initiatives in the district to counteract discrimination and oppression and to work towards service user/carer empowerment in other aspects of service provision. In doing so, the team has focused on social work policy, legislation and practice. The following are illustrations of our work in this area:

- The team has revised its practice in relation to reviewing care packages with an emphasis on social workers collaborating with service users in evaluating the quality of the services received from the social services department.

- The district has a number of service users currently accessing Direct Payments. The Adult Team is currently working on the extension of Direct Payments to older people, which will enable older people to organise and pay for their own care, thus providing them with choice and control which would otherwise not be available.

- Following the introduction of the Carers (Recognition and Services) Act 1995, the social services department began to consult with carers about their service needs. The carers identified the need for a 'sitting service' to enable them to have short breaks. The department used Carers Act money and worked in collaboration with Age Concern, the Carers Support Service and the Alzheimer's Disease Society to provide a sitting service for carers. Carers are able to choose when they want to access the service.

- Recent policy and legislation have concentrated on the need to work in partnership with health and housing professionals in order to provide preventive and rehabilitation services (see Chapters Four and Five). The district now provides support from health, housing and social services working together to provide assessment and rehabilitation for older people to enable them to make more informed decisions about their future accommodation.

This chapter began by stating that the team wished to consider the rhetoric of empowerment against the reality of practice. Writing this chapter has provided the authors with an opportunity to revisit the literature on empowerment and partnership and to make sense of the recurring themes and issues. However, when it came to applying the insights from the 'high ground' of theory to the 'messiness, complexity, ambiguity and uncertainty of day-to-day reality for practitioners', the themes and issues became much more complex (Thompson 2000, p.152). In reality empowerment as a participative process is fraught with obstacles, as a result of tensions and dilemmas rooted in legislation and policy. Limited resources, priority systems and eligibility criteria have the potential to impinge on positive interventions by practitioners. Despite this constraining context, the chapter has shown that it is possible for practitioners to improve practice in community care. By working in partnership with services users and carers and encouraging their participation in all aspects of the social work process, empowerment need not be just a gesture. It may be the case that fundamental political change is needed for practice to be truly empowering at all levels of social work policy and practice, but this does not prevent individual practitioners from attempting to ensure that, as far as possible, 'their own work enshrines the value of partnership' (Thompson 2000, p.136).

Notes

1   This is a team serving adults in a large rural area, with only 2 per cent unemployment. Although the area is considered to be affluent, some service users experience rural poverty and many service users experience difficulties related to living in a rural area, such as lack of public transport and the additional high costs of travelling to and from services.

2   There are no Black communities in the district and the Black population is 0.07 per cent.

3   As a result of our interviews, one service user, 'J', became more closely involved in the study. His experiences of social work intervention over a twenty-four-year period provided us with an historical insight into changes of attitude and philosophy within social services.

Chapter Seven

Partnership in Prevention
Messages from Older People

Denise Tanner

Introduction

This chapter is based on a small-scale research project concerned with older people who had referred themselves, or agreed to referral, to a social services department for some sort of help but had been told that they were not 'eligible' to receive a service. The study set out to explore how the older people managed their 'unmet need', ranging across their personal strategies to cope with difficulties, the help they received from family and friends and the use made of statutory and independent sector services.

Twelve older people who had been refused a service were interviewed on two separate occasions, approximately five months apart. Seven participants were female and five male, their ages ranging from 74 to 90. As well as participating in interview discussions, some of the older people also completed a diary, recording difficulties they experienced, how they set about dealing with them and their feelings about the effectiveness of these strategies. In this way the study was concerned not only with the 'facts' of what help was received or not received, but also with older people's perceptions and feelings about their situations. The aim was to find out what they found helpful in managing their difficulties and where the 'gaps' were in terms of problems they were not able to resolve. Such understanding has the potential to inform the development of preventive strategies for older people.

The chapter will outline key aspects of the policy context which are pertinent to the study before discussing some of the main findings and links to other research evidence. The latter part of the chapter will draw out the implications of the issues raised for the development of preventive strategies and services.

Policy context

Three issues are important in understanding the context to the study. These are:

- the application by local authorities of 'eligibility criteria' when deciding who is entitled to receive a service
- growing recognition of the benefits of a more preventive approach for both service users and providers
- an increased emphasis on the importance of listening to the voices of older people themselves.

'Eligibility criteria'

The community care reforms of the early 1990s were based on the stated aims of enabling people to live in the community for as long as possible and of promoting people's independence and choice (Department of Health 1989). Those in difficulty would receive a 'needs-led' assessment that would enable services to be tailored to their individual requirements (Social Services Inspectorate 1991b). However, following the implementation of the reforms, local authorities have faced both an increased demand for their services and financial constraints. This has meant they have had to restrict the services they provide to keep within their budgets. Following central government guidance, they have done this by setting 'eligibility criteria' which enable them to regulate service provision in line with the resources they have available. As their financial resources diminish, they are able to tighten their eligibility criteria so that fewer people 'qualify' for a service. 'Need' is defined in the context of the local authority's resources rather than by a fixed normative definition of need or by the expressed needs of service users (Tanner 1998). The declared intention, at the time of the reforms, of separating 'need' from 'services' thus becomes not just blurred but indistinct in what has been described as '...a masterpiece in the art of circle-squaring' (Lewis and Glennerster 1996, p.15).

In practice, this means that the people who meet social services departments' eligibility criteria are those who are most frail and at risk and who would be unable to remain in their own home unless services were provided. Social workers are reduced to providing 'a service of last resort' (Langan 1993, p.163), rather than the comprehensive and preventive services envisaged at the time of the Seebohm Report (Harris 1999; White and Harris 1999). A number of studies have attested to services being concentrated on 'crisis' and 'survival' needs at the expense of the promotion of quality of life (see, for example, Ellis 1993; Richardson and Pearson 1995; Stanley 1999).

One example of this change in emphasis in the services provided is that of home help. This used to include the provision of domestic cleaning for a large number of older people. Following the renaming of the service as 'home care' it is largely if not exclusively restricted to those requiring assistance with personal care tasks such as washing and dressing. National statistics show the continuing shift to the provision of a more intensive service to a smaller number of households, as indicated by increases in the number of contact hours per household mirrored by a continuing fall in the number of households receiving home care. The proportion of households receiving only one visit of two hours per week or less, for example, has decreased from 42 per cent in 1992 to 21 per cent in 1999 (Department of Health 2000c). Thus home care provides one example of eligibility criteria being used to direct scarce resources to people in greatest need. However, there are clearly implications for the larger number of people who fall outside the criteria and who are refused a service.

Prevention

A report by the Audit Commission (1997) highlighted the 'vicious circle' of provision in which services focused on 'high-level' needs consume large amounts of resources leaving few available for preventive and rehabilitative work. Wistow and Lewis (1997) see prevention as having two main components: preventing or delaying the need for more expensive services and promoting older people's quality of life and participation in the community. The first of these is identified by Fletcher (1998) as the cost-effectiveness case for prevention and the second as the consumer case. While the two are inter-linked, agencies may be more concerned with the cost-effectiveness aspects of prevention while older people may be more concerned with quality of life issues.

Health and social care policy documents are increasingly acknowledging the need for a shift in emphasis from services targeted at situations of 'high-risk' to 'lower-level' provision (Department of Health 1998a). A new 'Promoting Independence' prevention grant has been allocated to local authorities to stimulate the development of preventive strategies. It seems many local authorities are using this to develop rehabilitation and reablement schemes directed at preventing further deterioration in already 'high-risk' groups, for example, those being discharged from hospital or on the threshold of residential care. This is where, in the shorter term at least, the cost-effectiveness case may be most evident. A systematic review of the literature on low-intensity practical support services carried out by Quilgars (2000) concludes that while the cost-effectiveness case for low-level prevention has still to be made, there is some evidence in relation to the 'consumer case'. Research by Langan, Means and Rolfe (1996) demonstrates the psychological significance of 'home' for older people and the importance of services enabling them not only to remain in their homes but also to participate in activities and social relationships and keep up their usual routines. Similarly, studies by Clark, Dyer and Horwood (1998) and Bartlett (1999) show that services such as help with housework, gardening, shopping, laundry and household repairs and maintenance are of prime importance to older people. These 'quality of life' aspects of prevention may shed further light on what older people themselves require from 'preventive' services.

Listening to the voices of older people

If preventive strategies are concerned with quality of life as well as cost-effectiveness, it is vital that the experiences and perceptions of older people themselves inform their development. Much research has been carried out *on* older people, rather than *with* them, has ignored the meaning their experiences have for them and has denied them a part in defining their own needs (Gearing and Dant 1990). Some research studies tend to push older people to the sidelines, perhaps because it can seem easier to communicate with 'carers' than with older people themselves (Baldwin 1996; Myers and MacDonald 1996).

Recent policy initiatives require agencies to be more accountable to those who use their services. The *Modernising Social Services* White Paper (Department of Health 1998a), for example, requires local authorities to carry out surveys to gauge levels of satisfaction among service users and family carers. While this gives positive support to the argument that the views of older people who are service users must be sought, it does not give a voice to the growing numbers of older people denied a service. This is a significant omission since there is the potential to learn much about prevention from those who are 'coping' without support from the state.

Study themes

Having considered key aspects of the policy context, some of the main findings of the study are discussed here in terms of recurring themes arising in the discussions with the older people.

'I struggle but I'm getting by': older people's efforts to 'keep going'

A strong theme that emerged was that of 'keeping going'. Participants talked about their efforts to continue living their lives in their usual ways. This encompassed a number of themes concerned with preserving continuity and maintaining important routines and relationships, including:

- doing things for themselves and not having to rely on other people
- continuing to live in their current home
- 'making ends meet' financially
- being able to get out and about
- keeping up hobbies, interests and relationships.

These themes are akin to those identified by Langan *et al.* (1996) in their study of factors important in enabling older people to maintain their independence. To give a few examples from the current study, 'getting by' for Mrs King[1] was linked with maintaining her usual social activities, and 'putting on a brave face' so that her relationships with friends would not be altered by their awareness of her problems. For Mrs Forrester (who is in her 90s), staying active was the key feature of 'keeping going' and this was seen as essential in preventing her from becoming 'old'.

For many of the participants, 'keeping going' had become more difficult because of problems linked with illness or disability:

> When you've got these ailments, I mean, it's all right getting old, but it's what comes with it, and when you've got these ailments, instead of sitting and moaning about them, you've sort of got to take things easier, but you have got to get up and go and have some exercise…I do my own shopping. I usually do it each day because I've been warned not to carry heavy bags, and if I do, believe me, I know about it…if I get potatoes or milk or anything like that, I take the trolley. I struggle but I'm getting by. (Mrs King)

All of the participants showed a high level of resourcefulness and creativity in the strategies they used to manage their difficulties:

> One of the things I find extremely difficult is changing the bed because I can't bend over so I do it all on my hands and knees… There are things like that I do find very difficult but I do cope…I am so used to doing things on my hands and knees, like dusting or anything at floor level, that I just do it, so it means doing things one-handed. Quite often I've cut the edges of the

lawn with a pair of scissors because I can't cope with shears you see. (Mrs Manders)

Some tasks that were once accomplished easily were now an effort so that 'keeping going' inevitably involved 'struggle'. However, this struggle was seen as essential for maintaining independence. Mrs Manders, for example, talked of her exhaustion after she had persevered in mowing her lawn:

> I realise now that those sorts of jobs are very difficult for me... if I'm feeling OK I shall still [do them] because... if you give up doing these things then you lose your independence entirely. (Mrs Manders)

Help was only sought from outside sources when the struggle became impossible to continue or the costs (for example, risk to health) were seen as too great and when the difficulty in question was seen as essential to 'keeping going'. When this point was reached, the older people were looking for support to supplement their own efforts and address those tasks that they could not do for themselves.

Participants appeared to have a clear idea of what they could manage, what they found difficult and – in most cases – what help they would like. They were looking to social services to provide this specific help. This is supported by Richards' (2000) study of social work assessments of older people which found that the majority of people entered the assessment process 'decided', that is, with a clear view of their difficulties and the response they wanted. Assessment and care management are founded on the notion of professionals working with service users to first, identify their 'needs' and second, decide on the most appropriate services to meet those needs (Social Services Inspectorate 1991b). Research suggests that practice often departs from this. First, assessment is still often led by workers' knowledge of available services rather than by identified 'needs' (Baldwin 2000; Davis, Ellis and Rummery 1997). Second, service users may have little say about either which needs are met or which services are put in place to address them (Myers and MacDonald 1996).

'No one ever died from having a dirty floor': accessing help from social services

Since being refused services by social services was one of the criteria for inclusion in the study, it was not surprising to find that participants experienced a mismatch between their view of the help needed and what was available from social services. Two frequently cited examples were bathing and cleaning. In common with many local authorities, neither of these was defined by the participating authority as 'necessary', unless there were specific health or hygiene reasons for the help being given. For the participants, however, being able to maintain their bodies and/or their homes to what they perceived to be an acceptable standard was of crucial significance:

> ...I got a letter and it listed four disabilities and it said if you don't have any of them you don't meet our criteria, and I didn't...the upshot of it is I can't have it. I do not understand it... Normally I like to bath every morning, now I can't and I feel dirty. (Mrs Forrester)

Other studies have shown the emotional and symbolic significance of bathing (Twigg 1997) and maintaining household standards, particularly for women (Clark, Dyer and Horwood 1998). For some of the participants, it was not that no help was offered from social services, but that the help offered did not accord with their view of the support they needed. Mrs Anderson, for example, had severe osteo-arthritis and continence problems. She preferred to manage her personal care herself, even though it could take her two hours to get washed and dressed in the mornings. She asked social services for help with the heavy cleaning, but was told she could only have help with personal care, which she refused:

> Someone from social services came and said they don't help with cleaning now because no one ever died from having a dirty floor.

Following heart surgery, Mr Williams was allowed a home carer to do shopping for him but not help with the cleaning:

> They are not allowed to do cleaning and that is what I needed them to do. I had to pay...and I thought I can't afford to pay for this when it is no good to me so I stopped it.

Any annoyance or disappointment about having been refused a service may, ironically, have been tempered by the view that the help may not have responded to their needs anyway. For example, Mrs King when discussing the local authority home care service said:

> They're not allowed to do this, they're not allowed to do that, so what's the good of paying them to do something you can do yourself, you want them to do the things you can't do...which will probably be things they aren't allowed to do...why bother with it?

'On a paying basis': accessing private help

The community care reforms aimed to encourage a 'mixed economy' of welfare so that 'consumers' could have choice from a range of services in the private and voluntary as well as the statutory sectors (Walker 1997). It is therefore of interest to explore how well served the study participants were by the private sector when refused statutory help.

Some of the study participants expressèd a preference for buying services privately as this allowed them control over the terms under which help was given. For example, Mrs Manders said:

> I find it very difficult to ask anyone to do anything actually, unless it's on a paying basis…I've always been used to doing everything for myself…I'm still trying to find someone to come in and help me, but I would rather have someone privately if I can who would do what I want, even if I said take me into [town] for a couple of hours, you know…I would like someone that could do what I would, what I need help with, and not just what they are allowed to do sort of thing…

Similarly, Wilson (1993) found in her study of older people that those able to buy services from the private sector were able to retain greater control of certain areas of their lives. Purchasing help did not create the same feelings of dependency as receiving 'care' based on their 'needs'.

However, although Mrs Manders and some of the other participants had the financial resources to buy help, they were hampered by a lack of information about services. The low level of knowledge and understanding about both statutory and independent sector services was a significant theme throughout the interviews, and this is a similar picture to that found in other studies (Clark, Dyer and Horwood 1998; Davis, Ellis and Rummery 1997; Richards 2000).

Another problem was the lack of local and appropriate provision so that even people who had the financial resources, confidence and skills to negotiate buying services were unable to make their own arrangements for meeting need. In Mrs Anderson's words:

> It's not paying that is a problem; it's finding the help. I've tried for ages to get help in the village but I can't find anyone.

Particularly disadvantaged were those people in outlying villages where there were no local agencies. If they managed to find an agency which covered their area, heavy additional travel costs were incurred. This highlights another issue, the dissatisfaction some participants felt about the terms under which private help was provided. The cost of the service is an obvious example, as illustrated by this comment from Mrs Anderson about a private domiciliary care agency that sent her information:

> Anyway, when I looked at the price list, it looked all right to start with but then it was plus VAT which I think is disgusting for people, to pay a service

charge you know, when it's for things people have to have. And it was 38 pence a mile for petrol plus VAT again.

Another issue mentioned by several participants was the practice some agencies had of sending a team of two or even three carers into the home. Mrs Thomas, who lived with her husband in a small flat, found the idea of this totally unacceptable. Mrs Wade gave it a try but was dissatisfied with the standard of work and found that the development of a personal relationship with a helper was more difficult because the two helpers tended to relate to each other, rather than to her. Also highlighting the significance of the relationship with the helper, a concern expressed by several participants was about allowing a 'stranger' into the home. As Mrs Manders said:

> …the older you are the more you feel you need someone you know rather than someone you don't know. It's worrying to have strangers coming into the house, I mean I know they're all checked and everything, it's just how you feel.

Some participants were fortunate in being able to find paid helpers through their social networks. By the time of the second interviews, two of the study participants who had been told that housework could not be provided by social services had managed to find someone to clean for them privately through their informal contacts. Even though these helpers may not have been previously known, they were not perceived as 'strangers' because there was a personal connection between them and someone in the older person's social network. Where these relationships existed they seemed to work well, giving people the feeling of control they would have in a market relationship, the sense of security associated with statutory provision and the feeling of familiarity associated with informal care, though without the sense of obligation:

> I pay this woman £35 a week and she comes and does my boilers and exercises the dogs and does the floor and any odd jobs that want doing around the place. She comes in twice a day, she comes in the evenings to see if I'm all right and that…she's good and she keeps everything nice for me. And then the garden was worrying me, and I got this woman…down the road, I asked her and she said, 'Well, you can explain what's got to be done and then I'll do it.' (Mr Jones)

Some 'informal' private arrangements could however prove fragile and unreliable:

> There's a young lad I pay to do the garden but he hasn't been lately. I don't know if it's because it's wet. I did try to get someone to do the housework

but nothing's happened. My friend, she contacted somebody and they said, yes, they were interested, but nothing happened. (Mr Norris)

Other participants were prevented from purchasing care through lack of financial resources. Inequality is 'one of the fundamental continuities of later life' (Thompson, Itzin and Abendstern 1990, p.244) and widening economic inequalities mean that unequal access to private care in later life is likely to increase rather than diminish. Recent evidence suggests that many older people lack sufficient incomes to meet even their basic needs (Parker 2000). Thus, expecting older people to function as consumers without ensuring they have the financial means to purchase care can be seen as 'just plain insensitive' (Baldock 1998, p.179).

It was also the case that some study participants were not equipped with other 'resources' necessary to access the market, in particular, requisite attitudes and values. Participants who had purchased goods they needed (for example, Mr Norris who had purchased a scooter and various disability aids privately) did not necessarily feel equipped to purchase care services via the market. Baldock and Ungerson's (1994) research highlights that obstacles to market use may be a matter of values and culture rather than facts and information. They term these 'habits of the heart' and indicate the barriers to purchasing help for those who have a history of low participation in the market. Mrs King did not have the financial resources to buy help but even if given additional income, she would not have had the knowledge, confidence or skills necessary to negotiate her own care arrangements:

> ...if I wanted a cleaner, I wouldn't know where to go to get one because I never let myself get that involved with things sort of thing. I just live, just a quiet life, day to day.

Although it is now possible in principle for older people who meet eligibility criteria to access Direct Payments so that they can purchase their own care, this will be inadequate if issues of information provision, support, confidence, skills and the availability of acceptable private provision are not also addressed. Direct Payments also, of course, do nothing to help the situation of those who fall outside eligibility criteria.

'Why should I put it onto them': accessing help from family and friends

Studies have found that people who have strong social support networks feel more positive about themselves and about their lives generally (Scott and Wenger 1995; Wenger 1984). The current study found that social networks are an important source of both information and helping resources for older people. Those people with fewer social relationships are likely to be at a disadvantage in terms of both knowing about services and having access to potential helpers. However, while support networks may be important in helping people to address their difficulties, the study findings warn against making assumptions about the support that people will be prepared either to give or to receive.

The study participants saw their relationships with family and friends as reciprocal, based on mutual support rather than on the notion of a help-giver and a help-receiver. Mrs Forrester, for example, gave help by looking after her grandchildren and repaid those who helped her with jars of homemade jam and chutney. She had an arrangement with a man across the road that he maintained, and kept the produce from, her vegetable plot and in return he tended her front garden free of charge.

Maintaining reciprocity in helping relationships can require careful management to preserve the self-esteem of all parties. Mr Williams described how others in the housing complex repaid him when he helped them:

> There is one…lady who can't read English well and she asks me to come over if she has any correspondence she can't understand and I explain it to her. Then, a day or two later, she will phone and ask me to go over and she will say, I was cooking and had some left over, here you are, and I say, right, thank you – she always has some left over! Another one, I helped her when the water was overflowing and she was flooded. She came round the next day with something she had bought too many of and would I like one.

There were other instances of what may be termed 'indirect' reciprocity, where it seemed that self-esteem could be preserved by helping others rather than necessarily the help-giver. Mrs Wade drove her older and frailer friend to the shops each week, while Mr Jarman raised small sums of money for charities by opening his garden to the public every summer.

A number of studies have shown that where people perceive their relationships with others as based on equality and mutual support, they feel more independent and more positive about themselves (Langan, Means and Rolfe 1996; Pratt and Norris 1994; Wenger 1984). Conversely, they feel more dependent when they see themselves as having nothing of value to exchange in relationships (Wilkin 1990). It is important to note that what is exchanged in relationships may be expressive rather than tangible. For example, although Mrs Anderson was physically limited in what she could do to support her daughter and son-in-law, who had a debilitating illness, she telephoned them every day to offer emotional support.

The study participants expressed a high level of concern about asking for help from their families and this has been found in other research involving older people (Clark, Dyer and Horwood 1998; Tulle-Winton 1999; Wenger

1984). They spoke in terms of there being 'boundaries' around help-seeking, that is, clear limits about what and how much it was acceptable to ask for and receive, and they were concerned not to transgress these boundaries. Mrs Manders saw being independent as about 'not needing to call on anyone, other than paid help', and she described her difficulty in asking for help:

> ...it's very hard for me, very hard. I feel a nuisance. I feel like I'm eternally apologising for being a nuisance, for saying can you do this for me, will you do that?

Precisely where these boundaries are drawn is different for each individual and each relationship, depending on its history, nature and context. Attitudes about helping boundaries were also affected by the perceived situation of the help-giver. Concern was expressed about accepting help from people who were seen as having their own problems, with a reluctance to 'add to the load'. As Mrs King said of her friends:

> ...they've got their own families, worries and troubles, so why should I put it onto them?

One of the stated aims of the community care reforms was the support of 'informal' carers (Department of Health 1989) and there were later developments aimed at improving the support provided, such as the Carers (Services and Recognition) Act (1995) and the National Strategy for Carers (Department of Health 1999c). However, evidence from the current study and other research suggests that those constructed as the recipients of care may prefer to receive help from sources other than family and friends (Minichiello, Browne and Kendig 2000). Wilson's (1993) research, based on interviews with people over the age of 75, found that statutory services were often seen as preferable to family help; professionals were seen as being paid for their work and this reduced the feelings of 'being a burden' that tended to accompany receipt of help from families. For those forced into the position of having to depend on families and friends there may therefore be a risk of loss of self-esteem and loss of perception of themselves as independent.

'Inside, I'm the same as I've always been': sustaining the self

A key theme in the way the participants attempted to manage their difficulties was their efforts to maintain a sense of their identity. Their personal strategies to 'keep going', determination to keep their helping relationships within certain boundaries and reciprocal and the search for external sources of help that would respond to their own definition of their needs can all be seen as part of a striving, often against opposing pressures, to sustain their sense of 'self' or 'who they are'. One study of people over the age of 80 also highlighted identity as a significant theme, defining this as '...that aspect of self and personality which expresses the overall unity and purpose of the individual's life' (Coleman, Ivani-Chalian and Robinson 1998, p.391).

Charmaz (1983) carried out interviews with people who were chronically ill. She found that it was difficult for them to keep a positive self-image when the experiences and meanings on which their positive identity had been based were no longer available. Charmaz sees illness as an assault upon the self and one of the most significant aspects of this assault as being 'the inability to control one's self and life in ways that had been hoped for, anticipated and assumed' (Charmaz 1983, p.187).

The study participants were all struggling to cope with the effects of some level of disability and/or ill health. The consequences of these difficulties had changed some fundamental aspects of their lives on which their positive identities had been based. Mr Norris, for example, no longer visited his local social club because of deterioration in his physical mobility, speech (following a stroke) and hearing. Mrs Anderson had stopped inviting people back to the house because she was worried about not being able to keep it clean. Mrs Manders had been used to giving her friends lifts on their outings and felt that her life was drastically changed when she was forced to give up driving:

> It's just left me completely stranded. I've always been so used to doing everything for myself and going everywhere, it's just completely transformed my life and I haven't yet got it sorted out.

In addition to the very real practical concerns associated with the difficulties the participants experienced (such as not being able to have a bath, not being able to maintain the garden), these difficulties had a deeper significance in that they threatened people's positive views of themselves. They looked for ways of resisting the threats to identity and of holding on to positive self-images.

These findings have considerable significance for the development of effective preventive services. They show that attention is needed not only to *what* services are provided but also *how* they are provided. A useful distinction is made by Bury (1991) between 'strategies', that is the actions people take to deal with their difficulties, and 'coping', that is, the personal implications and meanings that these may have. To illustrate this by an example, arranging for family members to give help to an older person may be a useful strategy in helping to address some of the practical difficulties, but it may not help people 'cope' (that is, give them positive feelings about their situation) if it makes them feel dependent and a burden. Similarly, services may deal with practical tasks but undermine people's sense of 'coping', if they are provided in a way that does not support that person's sense of positive identity.

Mr Robbins found himself in this situation. He had moved from the North into sheltered accommodation to be closer to his family, which was very caring and concerned for him, providing both practical and emotional support. However, although Mr Robbins had all of his physical needs met to a high level, he felt emotionally stifled and cosseted both by the confined nature of his accommodation and by the restricting anxieties of his family. He saw himself as someone who disliked being 'settled' but who liked to be 'free', mobile (moving house every three or four years) and active. This image of himself was difficult to maintain partly because of the deterioration in his physical health but more significantly because he felt 'hemmed in' by his family's concern and their need to see him 'safe and settled'. This seems to be a situation where the actions to deal with needs (strategies) had addressed practical difficulties but at the expense of emotional and psychological needs (coping).

Good practice in prevention: implications of the study's findings

It will be apparent that what has been reported here is a small-scale study based on interviews with a few older people. There are a number of possible factors influencing both who was invited to participate in the study and who agreed to participate, so the people interviewed cannot be seen as necessarily representative of all older people referred for help but refused a service. There was no attempt to seek a gender or class balance, for example. Also, it is important to remember that all of those interviewed are of white UK ethnicity. The intention is not to reach definitive conclusions but rather to try to draw out some key messages from the experiences of a small number of older people to help inform preventive strategies.

Monitoring and responding to 'unmet need'

Although assessment and care management guidance required local authorities to record unmet need so that this could be fed through to those responsible for planning services (Social Services Inspectorate 1991b), there has been a fear felt by local authorities that defining something as a 'need' may legally oblige them to meet it. This has led to subtle manoeuvres to obscure or redefine need (Lewis and Glennerster 1996). In reality, the

Gloucestershire judgement – that local authorities could take account of their resources in deciding whether it is necessary to meet need – clarified that it is lawful for unmet need outside the authority's criteria to be openly acknowledged (Schwehr 1999).

When trying to identify potential participants for the study, it was difficult to obtain clear information about situations where a decision had been made that people were ineligible for a service. This was partly because the computerised codes used to record the reason for 'closure' were not interpreted in a way that kept them conceptually distinct. For example, if someone who requested help with cleaning was sent a brochure listing private agencies, the reason for closure might be recorded as 'service not required', rather than 'not eligible for a service'. It is also likely that many people who feel in need of a service are no longer being referred to social services because key professionals such as GPs and district nurses, as well as members of the public, have been successfully re-educated about the operation of eligibility criteria.

Any meaningful monitoring of unmet need requires a clear, consistent and comprehensive mechanism of recording. This should encompass not only the recording by duty social workers of need which does not meet eligibility criteria, but also need identified by other professionals that they do not refer because of the restrictions they know exist on eligibility. These identifications of unmet need would assist the development of wider preventive strategies by highlighting areas where service provision may need to be directed or developed. (See Chapter Six for an example of the development of a befriending service, on the basis of informal monitoring of unmet need by social workers, to respond to the needs of people refered to the social services department as lonely and isolated, but who did not meet the eligibility criteria for social services.)

Building on strengths and existing coping strategies

The study has shown that older people are immensely resourceful in the strategies they use to try to manage their difficulties and that for the most part they are knowledgeable about their specific needs and the help they require to address them. They are not looking for services which 'take over' and remove all difficulties but for services which respond to the specific tasks they are no longer able to manage, even with struggle, or where the physical costs or risks of struggle are seen as too great. The key message from this for assessors and service providers is to treat people as experts in their own problem-solving and to seek to build on their existing strengths and strategies (Smale, Tuson and Statham 2000). Such an approach would ensure that the help provided supplements rather than supplants the older person's own efforts, sustaining their sense of self in the process.

Recognising that 'need' is defined by individuals in diverse ways

The older people in this study attached varying degrees of importance to different aspects of need and it has been suggested that this reflects their different sources of positive identity. A positive sense of self may, for example, be rooted primarily in having a clean house, maintaining a clean and well-groomed physical appearance, having a well-tended garden or in continued pleasure or success in a chosen hobby. Some or all of these areas may be deemed inessential from the perspective of agencies and professionals but as essential needs for the people concerned. A key assessment task is to determine with each individual the sources of her/his positive sense of self so that this can guide the intervention, alongside agency definitions of risk. This may mean being flexible about the implementation of eligibility criteria. For example, if someone is eligible for help with personal care but prefers to struggle to manage this on their own, 'eligibility' could be transferred to another area of self-defined need. This would allow a similar level of flexibility in statutory provision to that available through the Direct Payment scheme. Where social services are not able to provide the support indicated, such an approach would at least enable information and advice about relevant helping sources to be given.

Recognising the wider significance of practical tasks

Following on from the previous point, it has been shown that 'functional' tasks such as cleaning and gardening can have a deeper significance both in terms of their emotional and psychological value to people and in leading to indirect benefits, for example, a clean home serving to encourage social contact: 'The home is not simply a physical environment, it can encapsulate the public and private identity of the older person (Clark, Dyer and Horwood 1998, p.64). The consequences of not meeting these needs are therefore potentially greater than simply the non-completion of the task, for example, social isolation and depression. While it may be beyond the capacity of local authorities to meet lower-level needs within their limited budgets, it may be that low-cost initiatives in the independent sector can be developed and perhaps subsidised to address these areas.

Listening to people's stories

Treating people as experts in their own problems and responding to their specific needs means listening carefully to the 'stories', or narratives, that they tell about their lives (Richards 2000). The establishment of a relationship between the assessor and the older person is of prime importance for this to happen. It is difficult, if not impossible, to capture 'stories' if assessment is confined to predetermined frameworks or if information is only exchanged by telephone. Referral is often by someone other than the older person whose own account may be bypassed (Richards 2000). There are implications here for the way that both 'screening' and 'initial assessments' are carried out. Some of my interviews with the study participants uncovered different parts of the 'story' that had not been revealed in the referral or initial assessment – and the referral stage *is* often the initial assessment. Even where the assessment outcome (i.e. that the person is not eligible for services) remains the same, it is important to recognise the older person's perspective in the way the decision is communicated (Richards 2000). A one-off face-to-face dialogue based on an 'exchange' of information, as opposed to an assessment by telephone or via a third party, for example, (Smale and Tuson 1993) might prove an effective longer-term preventive measure. This would not necessarily be an additional task for social services but perhaps part of a service offered by a relevant local voluntary sector agency with the requisite knowledge and skills.

Reaching out

For older people, concepts of independence are linked with notions of 'doing things for oneself' and 'not relying on others' (Fisk and Abbot 1998). The participants set limits on their help-seeking and help-receiving to preserve their perception of themselves and their perception by others as independent. This means that in most cases, outside help is sought only with great reluctance. Evidence from this and other studies suggests that older people do not constitute a 'floodgate' of demand ready to open at the slightest opportunity. Instead, as the low take-up of means-tested welfare benefits by older people has shown, a proactive approach is required to encourage older people to access the help for which they are eligible. This is more likely to succeed where help is perceived as a right and 'open to all' (for example, access to a GP) than when that help is seen as part of a stigmatised, restricted and hard-to-access service.

Paying attention to how as well as what help is provided

This study has indicated that attention is needed by both assessors and service providers to *how* help is provided as well as *what* help is provided. It is possible for help to address identified practical difficulties but to undermine the positive identity of the older person in the process of service delivery. This point brings together a number of issues raised earlier such as the need to attend and respond to the person's own definition of needs and requirements and the significance of delivering help through the medium of a personal and positive relationship. Other studies have demonstrated the importance to service users of the quality of relationships with service providers, the establishment of trust and communication of respect being key ingredients (Harding and Beresford 1996; Henwood, Lewis and Waddington 1998).

Providing information

This study and others (Davis, Ellis and Rummery 1997; Langan, Means and Rolfe 1996; Richards 2000) have identified a lack of information about both statutory and non-statutory sources of help and how to access them. This hampers people's own problem-solving efforts and contributes to a sense of insecurity about how future difficulties will be managed. Findings from the study suggest that a priority for preventive strategies is the provision of clear, comprehensive, up-to-date and easily accessible information about a whole range of services, how they can be accessed and the terms and criteria by which they operate. This is part of giving people the resources they need to engage in their own problem-solving.

Ensuring people have the resources to access help

In addition to information, other resources needed by older people, if their problem-solving is to be successful, are access to appropriate services and the resources to use them. The first of these requires that there is a range of agencies from which services can be obtained on terms people find acceptable and the second requires older people to have the financial and other resources (skills, confidence, attitudes etc.) necessary to function as 'consumers'. The provision of information, though important, is insufficient in itself. Some people may need support to find and arrange help. This could be a short-term intervention, again not necessarily by social services, but one with long-term benefits in terms of prevention of deterioration and maintenance of quality of life.

Recognising and supporting social networks without making assumptions about helping activity

The study has highlighted the significance of social networks in the provision of information and in identifying helping resources. It is reasonable to assume, as eligibility criteria do, that those people without active social networks are more vulnerable. However, it should not be assumed that social networks necessarily imply helping relationships. The presence of meaningful 'helping' will depend upon the quality of the relationships, the ability of potential helpers to deliver the type of help needed and the willingness of the older person to accept help from these sources. The way in which family care arrangements are negotiated can reinforce or change people's identities (Finch and Mason 1993). The care preferences of the older person need careful and sensitive checking as much as the willingness of potential carers to give help. Older people's preferences not to receive help from family or friends are to be respected and not contravened if positive identities are to be sustained.

Community participation

It is important to look at a wide range of services when exploring prevention, not just those provided by social services. Some services that do not have prevention as their explicit aim may play a key role in helping older people to 'keep going'. It is important to take account of these as well as health and welfare services when considering preventive strategies (Lewis *et al.* 1999). Examples of such services from the current study include chemists offering home delivery of prescriptions; supermarkets operating their own bus service and help with packing and carrying shopping; locally based shops and post offices; frozen meal home delivery services; and local religious and social activities. Preventive strategies need to be based on a broad definition of 'community care' that is concerned with enabling participation in the community as well as with meeting needs for welfare services (Barnes 1997). This requires a 'joined-up' approach between public, independent sector and community services and activities.

Older people as resources as well as recipients

Being able to see oneself as a help-giver, as well as a help-receiver, emerged as important in maintaining people's identity, self-esteem and perception of themselves as independent. Sometimes this was achieved through reciprocal help-giving with family and friends and sometimes by more general help-giving in the community or through supporting 'good causes'. In this sense, help in a preventive sense is not just about what is received but also about what is given. Thornton and Tozer (1994) give a number of examples where older people are producers as well as consumers of services, for example, Village Care Groups, where many of the volunteers are older people, and a Good Neighbour Scheme in which one of the roles performed by older people is the staffing of a telephone help-line. Time banks are another example of projects based on the mutual exchange of services (Eaton 2000). Although several of the study participants had poor health and were limited in what they could do physically, most had some skill or resource that could be exchanged, whether a service (for example, sewing, giving lifts, simple DIY jobs, baby-sitting) or goods (such as jam, cakes, garden plants or even paintings and sketches). Creating opportunities for reciprocity in help-giving can meet emotional, psychological and social needs as well as practical ones.

Conclusion

The central argument emanating from the study is that the ways in which older people seek to manage their difficulties are related to their efforts to sustain a positive identity. What this identity comprises is unique to each individual, although there are some common themes. For many older people, a perception of themselves as independent is a central component of a positive identity. This leads them to make strenuous and creative efforts to manage their own needs from within their own resources. Where help is needed with essential aspects of their lives (and the definition of 'essential', it is argued, relates to those areas that impinge on identity), help is sought that will sustain a positive sense of self and not detract from it. Effective help-giving must in some way connect with and support the positive identity of the help-receiver. This applies whether the help is given by formal services or by family and friends.

Prevention is now on the policy agenda and this is an encouraging shift of emphasis for older people. However, a measure of effective prevention cannot rest on the narrow basis of cost-effectiveness alone but must encompass psychological and emotional as well as physical well-being. Otherwise, we may succeed in reducing objective indicators of need (such as rates of admission to residential or nursing homes) but at the expense of enabling people to maintain a positive identity. As physical and emotional/psychological well-being are intertwined, only strategies that address both can be deemed effective in the long term.

Note

1   Pseudonyms are used throughout

Chapter Eight

Guardianship

A Participative Approach

Nicolette Barry

Introduction

This chapter explores the role of Guardianship within the 1983 mental health legislative framework (Mental Health Act 1983[1]), as a method of empowering[2] service users. As this chapter was written at a time when the 1983 Mental Health Act was under review and a new Mental Health Act was due for publication, conclusions will be drawn about how this kind of empowering practice in relation to Guardianship can be taken forward using the new Mental Health Act. The work which is described in this chapter emerged from an initiative in the social services department aimed at encouraging teams working with adults to look at ways of developing good practice. As an approved social worker[3], I decided to examine the work of the mental health team, focusing specifically on Guardianship. The project enabled me to examine in detail individual Guardianship Orders undertaken not only by my own mental health team, but also by teams across the department.

As Dalrymple and Burke point out, 'the functions of the law can be seen to have contradictory elements ... but can offer the opportunity to provide good practice' (Dalrymple and Burke 1995, p.26). In particular, the law can be used to benefit and empower service users. Guardianship has been a misunderstood and under-utilised part of the current mental health legislation, as can be seen by the number of Guardianship Orders used over the last decade as compared with other sections of the 1983 Mental Health Act. (See Table 8.1.)

Table 8.1 Comparison of use of Orders (Mental Health Act 1983)		
	1987	*1997*
Number of Section Two Orders	8868	12,405
Number of Section Three Orders	2564	9200
Number of Guardianship Orders	123	376

(Compiled from Department of Health 1997c, 1998e).

There are many publications, in particular the biennial reports of the Mental Health Act Commission (1983–1995), which highlight a number of reasons why social workers have resisted using Guardianship Orders. Such Orders have been seen as complex and cumbersome, paternalistic and controlling. They are considered to have resource implications, while also being perceived as lacking powers, and as having the disadvantage of being able to be removed or discharged by the nearest relative. Many social workers see Guardianship as working against social work principles of user empowerment, participation and partnership. Some social workers argue that Guardianship contains a 'Catch 22' element. If there is a good relationship with a service user, then powers over her/him are not needed. If a relationship cannot be established with a service user, then the powers under a Guardianship Order, which rely on user involvement, will not work. The chapter challenges these criticisms of Guardianship through the use of two case studies. The case studies illustrate that Guardianship can not only enable service users to remain living in the community, but also can improve their quality of life and extend the range of options available to them. The chapter concludes by looking at the lessons which can be learnt from the way Guardianship has been utilised by social workers to empower clients and how those lessons can be taken forward in the era of the implementation of the new Mental Health Act.

The history of Guardianship

In order to understand Guardianship it is important to understand its history, its original role in mental health legislation and how it has developed. Guardianship first appeared in mental health legislation in the Mental Health Act (1959). Its alleged goal was to control people with severe mental impairments (Graham *et al.* 1990). Graham argues that this allegation can be substantiated by the number of people with severe mental impairments who were on Guardianship Orders under the 1959 Act, as compared with those under the jurisdiction of the Mental Health Act (1983). In 1967, under the 1959 Mental Health Act, over 60 per cent of those under a Guardianship Order had a mental impairment compared to only 20 per cent in 1983 under the 1983 Mental Health Act (Hughes 1990). The figures used in Hughes' article show that there is a continued trend in the use of Guardianship away from service users with severe mental impairments towards those with a range of other mental disorders. It will be shown later that this was particularly true of the way in which Guardianship was used within Warwickshire. Of the seven people on Guardianship Orders at the time of writing this chapter, none of them had a severe mental impairment. However, this early emphasis on the use of Guardianship as a way of controlling people with severe mental impairments is one of the reasons why many social workers have regarded Guardianship as being paternalistic.

After Guardianship's appearance in the Mental Health Act (1959), there was pressure from various quarters, in particular from the Butler Committee[4] (Butler 1975) to change this section of the Act. This committee, along with pressure groups such as MIND (Gostin 1975), wanted to widen the scope of Guardianship away from its narrow focus on people with severe mental impairments. This support for widening the use of Guardianship occurred in a period when there was a speeding up of the process of closure of long-stay hospitals and the development of community care for service users with long-term care needs. In addition, there was a growing awareness of an increase in the population of older people, which brought with it an increase in the number of people with dementia, living in the community (Henwood 1992).

It was against the background of these developments that Guardianship took on its current format, as laid down in the Mental Health Act (1983). When comparing the 1959 Act with the 1983 Act, the major change is the narrowing down of the powers in the latter in order to make them more specific. The 1959 Act talked about the Guardian having the same powers as a 'father over a child of 14', which suggested a Guardian was in a powerful relationship with the service user. The 1983 Act is much more specific about what the powers of a Guardian are (see next section) and these are limited in their scope. Millington (1989) argues that one of the reasons for this was that there had been concerns when the 1983 legislation was being drawn up that Guardianship had been under-utilised in the 1959 Act. This under-use was thought to have been due to the lack of clarification of the powers under the 1959 Act and the overarching controlling paternalism of the guardianship section of this act, which made social workers wary of using it.

The changes made in 1983 were seen as making Guardianship easier to operate.

Millington also argues (on p.7–8)that the reason for the delineation of limited powers was connected with potential resource implications for local authorities. This can be illustrated by the Mental Health Act Commissioners Biennial Reports (1983–1995) in which approved social workers argued that Guardianship Orders were being under-utilised owing to their local authorities' fears concerning the implications for resources. The costs associated with Guardianship Orders will be examined in the case studies later. A further reason for the provision of limited powers in the 1983 Act may have been the lack of specific sanctions if a person defaults on a Guardianship Order. The only sanctions available are to detain the person under another section of the Mental Health Act (1983) and to take them into hospital. This goes against the aim of Guardianship, which is to keep the person in the community.

In sharp contrast to the idea that Guardianship has limited powers is a piece of case law. In the case of R. v. Kent County Council (1997) the court took the view that Guardianship Orders had a wide scope. The court agreed that a Guardianship Order gave the local authority the right to conceal a service user's address from a relative and to restrict mail sent by that relative, in the belief that this was in the best interests of that service user. The Kent County Council case illustrates how the court interpreted the Act as being wider in scope than was originally envisaged, and as having the potential to protect service users to a greater degree.

Since Guardianship developed into its current format, following the Mental Health Act (1983), it has remained, in my view, an infrequently used section of the Act (see Table 8.1). Even when comparing local authorities with similar population sizes and service user group sizes, there are great differences in the number of Guardianship Orders being used by local authorities (Department of Health 1997c). This supports Millington's conclusion concerning the degree of use of Guardianship, namely that it depends on approved social workers' commitment to using it, as laid down in the Code of Practice (Department of Health 1999e) and social services departments' willingness to take on the role of Guardian.

The new Mental Health Act, which is due for implementation by the end of 2002, does not contain a separate Guardianship Order. Instead, the Act includes what are referred to as Community Orders, which will be discussed later on in the chapter, but which still retain some of the aspects of the current Guardianship Orders. Although, Guardianship as a specific section will disappear, some aspects of it will continue in the new Mental Health

Act, as I hope will some elements of practice, which have been developed to empower service users.

What is Guardianship?

The aim of the Mental Health Act (1983) was to bring together the legislation related to people with mental health problems in order to manage effectively the care and treatment of 'mentally disordered patients' (Department of Health 1983, Section 1 [1]). In addition to the Mental Health Act (1983), memoranda pertaining to the Act (Department of Health 1999d), the Code of Practice (Department of Health 1999e), the National Assistance Act (1948) and case law (R. v. Kent County Council 1997) have implications for Guardianship. Section 1 of the 1983 Act provides a definition of 'mental disorder' and of those people to whom the Act can be applied. Sections 2 to 4 comprise powers which can be used to admit compulsorily service users into hospital, either for assessment (Section 2) or for treatment (Section 3). Section 4 deals with emergency admissions to hospital in circumstances in which only one medical recommendation is available. Sections 7 (Guardianship) and 25 (Supervision Orders) are concerned with powers that can be applied to patients outside hospital and are often referred to as the Community Orders.

The implementation of a Guardianship Order is clearly laid down both in the Mental Health Act (1983) (Jones 1999) Section 7, and the Code of Practice Section 13 (Department of Health 1999e). Although the Code is not a legally binding document, it is important as a statement of service users' rights and in promoting consistency across the country in the way that the Act is implemented. A service user can be received into Guardianship if s/he has

> attained the age of 16 years...is suffering from a mental disorder, being mental illness, severe mental impairment, psychopathic disorder or mental impairment and his mental disorder is of a nature or degree which warrants his reception into guardianship...and it is necessary in the interests of the welfare of the patient or for the protection of other persons that the patient should be so received. (Mental Health Act 1983, Section 7 [1–2])

The criteria for Guardianship are wide. They can be applied to most service users who are assessed under the Mental Health Act (1983) and therefore Guardianship should be considered when carrying out any Mental Health Act assessment. If social workers are endeavouring to practise within the ethos of the least restrictive alternative, as laid down by the 1983 Act, a

Community Order such as guardianship is less restrictive than a compulsory admission to hospital.

When considering Guardianship as part of a mental health assessment, a social worker needs to consider the appropriateness of the powers it provides in the context of the various options open for a service user in her/his particular circumstances. The powers of the Guardian, conferred on the Guardian by the Secretary of State via the local authority, are as follows:

(a) the power to require the patient to reside at a place specified by the authority or person named as Guardian;

(b) the power to require the patient to attend at places and times so specified for the purposes of medical treatment, occupation, education or training;

(c) the power to require access to the patient to be given at any place where the patient is residing, to any registered medical practitioner, approved social worker or other person so specified.

(Mental Health Act 1983, Section 8 [1a,b,c])

Once it has been decided by the approved social worker and the medical professionals involved in the mental health assessment to go ahead with a Guardianship Order then the next stage is to decide on the applicant. According to the 1983 Act, it is possible for either an approved social worker or the nearest relative (as defined in Section 28 of the Act) to make an application for a person to be placed under a Guardianship Order, with the support of two medical recommendations. On most occasions the person making the application is the approved social worker who has been asked to carry out a mental health assessment. S/he will approach the social services department to accept the service user on to a Guardianship Order. This part of the process is different from that contained in other sections of the Act, in that in this section the approved social worker or nearest relative has to approach the local authority, which then makes the decision about whether to place someone on a Guardianship Order. According to the Biennial Reports (Mental Health Act Commission 1993–1995) this is one of the reasons why some social workers avoid Guardianship, as they feel it is too cumbersome and bureaucratic. However, it is difficult to see how it could be processed differently in that Guardianship affects directly the local authority making the Order. The social services department has to provide resources to the individual under the Order, even if this is only providing someone to visit on a monthly basis.

Once a Guardianship Order is in place, it can last for up to six months (Mental Health Act 1983, Section 20[2]). At this point it should be reviewed. However, the Guardianship Order can be discharged at any point during the Order on application to a mental health tribunal by any regis-tered medical practitioner, by the responsible social services authority, by the service user's nearest relative or by the service user.

The possibility of discharge by the nearest relative is often seen as a weakness of Guardianship, in that many service users who can benefit from Guardianship are those who are vulnerable and being abused. Research has shown that vulnerable adults, particularly those suffering from dementia, are often abused by the nearest relative or another close family member (Gelles and Strauss 1979). The cause of this type of abuse was thought primarily to be due to the nature of the caring role. However, more recent work in this area (Bennett, Kingston and Penhale 1997) has shown that financial and environmental factors (low income and poor housing) are more likely to lead to abuse by carers. I would agree with this research and argue that from my experience the fact that a Guardianship Order is put in place, combined with use of the social services department's vulnerable adults policy, tends to highlight the abuse. This in turn often stops the abuse because it is now visible and because the carer, who is often the abuser, is now getting more support. This support can be in practical measures, such as carrying out a benefits check, which can immediately change the financial circumstances of both the carer and service user. My experience has also shown that it is very rare for the nearest relative to discharge an order when there is sus-pected abuse and there is in any case the option of discharging the nearest relative (Mental Health Act 1983, Section 23), if it is felt that s/he is not acting in the best interests of the service user.

Guardianship in one local authority

As an approved social worker in a social services department, I observed at first hand both the department's and social workers' commitment to using all parts of the Mental Health Act (1983). The department had produced its own policy and procedural guidelines on the use of Guardianship in order to ensure consistency. Much of the policy contained in the documentation reflected both the Act itself and the Code of Practice. The policy stated that: 'Guardianship is designed to improve the quality of life of persons with a mental illness or a mental handicap by enabling them to live in the commu-nity, when otherwise they might need to be hospitalised under compulsory procedures' (Warwickshire Social Services Department 1998, p.16). In the guidelines, Guardianship was presented as being a positive alternative to compulsory admission to hospital. Social workers were encouraged to consider this option for all service users when carrying out mental health assessments. The procedures outlined exactly how social workers should implement the legislation. They detailed what was expected of the local authority and of individual social workers, for example, the minimum number of visits per week. This enabled the approved social worker to be aware of the level of services they could offer to a service user, when considering Guardianship as an alternative to hospital admission.

It is clear from the policy and procedures that Warwickshire was committed to using Guardianship and this is reflected in the fact that in 1997 there were five service users on Guardianship Orders which compared favourably with many larger authorities. Oxfordshire, for example, had six Guardianship Orders in the same period (Department of Health 1997c). The even spread of Orders across the county covered by the social services department reflected the awareness and willingness of approved social workers throughout the authority to see this section of the Act as a realistic alternative to compulsory admission to hospital for service users. In my own district there were two people on Guardianship Orders and an account of their circumstances follows, along with a discussion on the issues raised and how these were dealt with by using Guardianship.

Mrs Smith[5]

Mrs Smith was a 64-year-old woman, who had been diagnosed with schizophrenia in her late 30s. She had never accepted this diagnosis and was erratic in taking her mediation. Since her divorce, Mrs Smith had been given a succession of council accommodation. When she was ill she would abandon her accommodation either to sleep rough or to move in with her 94-year-old mother. While sleeping rough, Mrs Smith had been attacked and her general physical and mental health had deteriorated due to lack of food and medication.

Over the years, Mrs Smith's children had approached social services for support for their mother and various attempts had been made over this time to try and engage with Mrs Smith, with little or no success. The latest contact with social services was from Mrs Smith's ageing mother, who felt that she could no longer cope with Mrs Smith staying with her and was afraid to tell Mrs Smith this. At the same time as Mrs Smith's mother contacted social services, Mrs Smith was found by the police wandering around a railway station in a distant town, having cycled over 50 miles to see her son. In fact, Mrs Smith had not seen her son for over 14 years, as he refused to see her and he no longer lived in that town. As a consequence, Mrs Smith was taken to the police station as a place of safety (Mental Health Act 1983, Section 146). A mental health assessment was then requested and she was placed on a Section 2 for assessment and taken back to her local psychiatric hospital.

Later this was converted to a Section 3 for treatment. While in hospital, Mrs Smith appeared to thrive. She was engaging with the staff and was willing to take medication. Her general physical and mental health was improving and she appeared to be happy with staying in the hospital.

As Mrs Smith became well, a Section 117[6] meeting was called by her psychiatrist to consider with other professionals, her family and Mrs Smith herself how best to maintain her in the community. A risk assessment had been carried out under the Care Programme Approach guidelines[7] (Dube 1997) and this was used as a basis for discussion in the meeting. The risk assessment showed that there were two main areas of concern about Mrs Smith living in the community. First, that Mrs Smith would return to alternating between sleeping rough and living with her mother, the latter being detrimental to her mother's health as well as her own. It was clear that were Mrs Smith to return to this lifestyle, her own mental and physical well-being would deteriorate. This could lead to further admissions to hospital, as well as placing her at risk of further abuse. Second, it was believed that Mrs Smith would not comply with treatment once back in the community. She still did not accept that she had a mental health problem. However, in hospital she had been willing to take medication because it was given to her, along with repeated explanations of its purpose. The effect of not taking treatment again was likely to be further deterioration in her mental health and repeated admissions to psychiatric hospital.

In the meeting, Mrs Smith made it clear that she wanted to live in the community with minimal involvement from services and she wanted to avoid further admissions to hospital. Mrs Smith was aware that when she was unwell she needed support, but was not able to ask for help owing to her illness. It was decided to apply for a Guardianship Order for Mrs Smith. The reason for this decision was that a Guardianship Order offered powers which would compel Mrs Smith to reside at her flat and would allow her to be returned to the flat by the police, if necessary. Further, it would give access to named workers to visit Mrs Smith at home and to try to encourage her to maintain her treatment.

After discharge Mrs Smith was regularly visited as outlined in the Guardianship Order and by the time of the six-monthly review meeting, it was clear that Mrs Smith was physically and mentally stable. Although she had left her flat on several occasions, she had been successfully returned by the police and she had allowed staff to visit her and to monitor her medication. In the review meeting, Mrs Smith made it clear that she wanted the Order to remain in place as she realised that it was helping her to remain well and had prevented any further admissions to hospital.

This set of circumstances illustrates one service user group, which can benefit from Guardianship, namely those service users who are unable to structure their own lives (Manning 1988; Watson 1996). A Guardianship Order enables such service users to have a structure or framework within which services can be delivered to them, while they retain some choices. Without this framework, many of them would move in and out of hospital, possibly with the end result of a move into residential care. In this sense, Guardianship is a partnership between the Guardian and the service user. A relationship is essential to this partnership, but unlike other areas of social work, the legal framework is also a fundamental part of that partnership. The Guardianship Order provides the framework in which the relationship takes place and gives the service user a structure to their lives, which they are not, at least at the time of the Order, capable of creating for themselves.

Mrs Edwards

The second case study illustrates the use of Guardianship with vulnerable adults. There are many service users who become vulnerable due to their mental health problems. One particular group of service users who are particularly at risk of abuse are those who suffer from dementia. The second case study illustrates how Guardianship can be used to protect service users at the same time as maintaining a level of freedom for them.

Mrs Edwards was a 90-year-old woman, who lived in a run-down cottage in an isolated village with poor amenities and had little contact with family or friends. Over the years that Mrs Edwards had lived in the village, her lifestyle had been that of a recluse and she came to be seen as an eccentric older woman. She began to be verbally abusive to local residents and her doctor asked for a mental health assessment to be carried out. The assessment was carried out in the community and although it was clear that Mrs Edwards was exhibiting bizarre behaviour, for example, wearing inappropriate clothing, such as wearing her nightdress during the daytime and going outside with no clothing on, it was thought that this was due to her personality and not due to a mental illness. As she was not considered to be suffering from a mental illness, it was not possible to place her under a section of the Mental Health Act. She was offered informal admission to hospital and support in the community, both of which she refused.

Although Mrs Edwards's behaviour continued to be abusive she remained in the community with support provided mainly by her doctor, whom she would allow to visit her. However, the situation deteriorated further, with Mrs Edwards experiencing a number of falls and being admitted repeatedly to the local hospital, but again refusing all offers of help on discharge. A nephew appeared and started to become involved in her care. He also refused any form of social services involvement. He provided her with no discernible support and was thought to be exploiting her financially. Mrs Edwards's short-term memory had declined, as had her ability to orientate herself in terms of time and place. Her consultant requested a psychiatric assessment during one of her admissions to hospital after a fall.

The psychiatric assessment concluded that she was suffering from a form of dementia and a mental health assessment was requested, as it was felt she was at risk of further falls and she was still refusing to accept help. A mental health assessment was carried out which found she was suffering from a mental illness and that she needed a period of assessment in hospital in order to protect her and to prevent further deterioration of her mental and physical health. Although her nephew was resistant to his aunt being admitted to psychiatric hospital he was forced by the consultant psychiatrist to see that she was at risk at home and that her health had deteriorated. Once the assessment was completed in psychiatric hospital and treatment was in progress, Section 117 discharge meetings were arranged to look at the risks to Mrs Edwards, together with the options available to her, when she was ready to go home.

The risk assessment highlighted various concerns including the likelihood of further injury owing to falls. It was believed that this was due to a combination of her poor mobility and the conditions in which she was living, for example, having to use an outdoor toilet. These problems could be reduced by alterations to her property and help from home care. It was also thought that her confusion between night and day might lead to her wandering out in the night in her night clothes into the road. This was considered not to be a serious concern due to the fact that she lived in a very isolated village and that the villagers would take her home if they saw her out late at night. However, there were concerns about the winter period and the possibility that she might develop hypothermia. The main concern at this time was her self-neglect which had been increasing due to her poor memory. She was forgetting to wash and eat, which meant that her physical health was deteriorating. Again it was felt that with home care, this risk could be diminished. Another concern was that her nephew was encouraging his aunt to refuse services and was thought to be taking money from her.

A number of options were considered, including returning Mrs Edwards to her home with an intensive support package or placing her in residential care. It was clear from the risk assessment that Mrs Edwards could be returned home with a support package, however there were concerns about her willingness to comply with the package. There was also concern that her nephew would disrupt the care package and continue to exploit his aunt financially, if she were to return home. The available powers under the Mental Health Act (1983) were then considered.

The consultant first suggested that Guardianship could be used to force Mrs Edwards to move into residential care. The approved social worker pointed out that this was not the case. Guardianship does not provide powers to transport service users into residential care and it is an order which is designed to keep people living as independently as possible in the community rather than moving them into residential care. There is no power to require that the person resides with a particular person in a particular place. Jones (1999, p.53) argues that the 'power to reside' was to discourage service users from sleeping rough, as with Mrs Smith, and not to move them into residential care. However, the updated Code of Practice does state that Guardianship can be used to provide the framework to enable service users to have their care needs met in a residential setting (Department of Health 1999e, p.56) This depends on their level of capacity. If they are incapable of making a decision regarding residential care, then a Guardianship Order can be made in order to provide a framework in which their care needs can be met and this can include providing the care in a residential setting. In these circumstances, another piece of legislation is required to move someone into the home in the first place as there are still no powers of transportation under Guardianship Orders.

However, I do believe that this addition to the new Code of Practice was made because of the increasing number of older service users with dementia, who can be seen by local authorities as draining their resources because of the amount of home care needed. The Bournwood judgement[8], although now overturned, also has implications in that many psychiatrists are now more willing to apply the Mental Health Act to older people, which in turn has enabled older people to access tribunals etc which were not available to them before. Prior to Bournwood, service users would not have been consulted about the move to residential care, due to their lack of capacity.

Mrs Edwards had the capacity to say that she did not want to go into residential care. Her nephew had made it clear that he would not support moving his aunt into residential care. This was thought to be because he was due to inherit the property, which she would have to sell if she went into residential care. There were ways in which risks could be reduced with help being given to Mrs Edwards at home, so it was felt that a Guardianship Order would provide the powers to gain access to Mrs Edwards in order for workers to provide support services and to monitor the situation. It was also hoped that the Guardianship Order would enable workers to monitor the financial abuse, which was suspected on the part of Mrs Edwards's nephew. Although Guardianship provides very little power in dealing with abusive situations, the fact that an Order is in place can be regarded by the abuser as someone officially watching them. In Mrs Edwards's case, this reduced the level of abuse. The nephew, as nearest relative, stepped back from being involved with his aunt as soon as the Order was in place and suddenly her money reappeared.

Mrs Edwards returned to live at home for about six months and she accepted care provided for her with some reluctance until, as her memory worsened, she became more acquiescent. Unfortunately, her mental health deteriorated to such an extent that it was considered that the risks (increased falls and wandering) were too great for her to remain living alone. A meeting was held with professionals, Mrs Edwards and her nephew and it was agreed that Mrs Edwards no longer had the capacity to make decisions regarding her future care and that she needed a more intensive care package than could be provided in the community. Her nephew was still against his aunt moving into residential care. He wrote to say he was taking action against the social services department, but when he was approached to discuss his views, he lost interest in the case. Mrs Edwards moved into a residential home and the Guardianship Order was removed.

This case study illustrates the use of Guardianship to protect someone who is vulnerable due to her or his mental health problems (Watson 1996). There are, of course, other social services polices such as vulnerable adults policies, but Guardianship is very specific in that it deals with adults with a mental health problem and this makes it a valuable tool in protecting service users, while enabling them to remain as independent as possible.

These two case studies illustrate types of service users who can benefit from the use of Guardianship Orders. Although they are a small group, their lives can be considerably improved by the use of Guardianship and for many of them the alternative would be long-term hospital admission or residential care. With structure and formalised support such service users have been able to maintain some independence and choice by living in the community for as long as their illness allows.

What is the future for Guardianship?

At the time of writing this chapter there are many changes occurring in the field of mental health services. Government initiatives such as *Building Bridges* (Department of Health 1995) and Partnership Programmes have meant that many social services and health departments have had to work more closely together. Mental health services are moving towards being provided by multi-disciplinary teams, with shared management by social services and health trusts. At the same time there are initiatives to develop specialist services to deal with certain service user groups, for instance, assertive outreach teams, whose aim is to work with service users who are difficult to engage in service provision. Alongside the service delivery changes, the government has also started to review the current Mental Health Act and we have already seen the influence of the new Code Of Practice (Department of Health 1999e) on the implementation of Guardianship Orders. The review of the Mental Health Act itself was led by an expert committee, whose role was to look at the current mental health legislation and then, in consultation with various interested groups, to put forward a new Act, which would 'reflect contemporary patterns of care within a framework which balances the need to protect the rights of individual patients and the need to ensure public safety' (Department of Health 1999b, p.1). In the review document which was published in November 1999, the expert committee put forward their proposals for changes to the Mental Health Act (Department of Health 1999b). Their main proposal was that the Mental Health Act should still focus primarily on compulsory admissions to hospital. However, there are various changes suggested in relation to the role of the nearest relative, tribunals and various other sections of the current Mental Health Act. The new Mental Health Act is based on the key principles of service user autonomy and participation. The treatment and care of service users should take place in the least restrictive environment and should ensure individual and public safety (Goodwin 1999, p.2).

Since the original report of the expert committee, there have been further changes to the new Mental Health Act through the publication of a White Paper in January 2001 (Department of Health 2001a). It is clear from the White Paper that Guardianship will not remain in its current form. The White Paper states that compulsory powers will replace all sections of the Act and that these compulsory powers can be used both in hospital and in the community, to ensure effective compliance with treatment (Winchester 2001). These changes will mean that service users will no longer be assessed under different sections of the Act, as there will be a single point of entry onto a compulsory care and treatment order. This care and treatment order could occur in the community as well as in hospital.

There are three important changes in the new Mental Health Act which are related to Guardianship.

Medication

Section 13 of the White Paper on Mental Health, states that 'care and treatment orders may apply to patients outside hospital' but there will 'be no powers for patients to be given medication forcibly, except in clinical settings. But steps will be specified in community orders to prevent patients, if they do not comply with their order, becoming a risk to themselves, their carers, or to the public'. Section 2.18 of the White Paper goes on to say, 'Compliance with treatment and contact with services will both be enforced under the new legislation in a way that was never possible under the 1983 Act.' This section also refers to the fact that hospital should not be used to 'ensure compliance with medication' and that this can be done in the community.

In these two sections, we can see reference to the idea of treating service users in the community. This is nothing new and was what Guardianship was about. The difference appears to be that Guardianship was based on the principle of partnership with a service user, as illustrated by the two case studies. The White Paper does not mention partnership in relation to compliance. Instead it implies that service users will be forced to take medication in 'clinical settings'. It is difficult to imagine how this will happen. I believe the reality will be that service users will be offered their medication at home and, if they refuse, will be threatened with being taken to hospital to be given their medication. The reason why I believe that service users will be forced to comply is from my own experience of home treatment teams, which are part of the government's reorganisation of mental health services. These teams go out to service users who are in crisis and offer medication. The service users know that if they refuse the team will arrange for a mental health assessment, which will probably result in admission to hospital, as there are few other alternatives to hospital care at present in the community. Clearly this is not what the review document in 1999 was referring to when it talked about 'user participation' (Department of Health 1999b). It seems that the emphasis is now more about control of service users for the safety of the public, rather than for the welfare of the service user.

The major concern with forcing service users to take medication is that not only does it remove their rights to choose their treatments, it also denies them the involvement in their treatment programme. Therefore, once the Order is removed they are more likely to be unwilling to engage with services which they see as a threat to their autonomy. At least with Guardianship Orders service users were aware of their rights and that it was a partnership, which, it was hoped, would go on after the Order was removed. This also enabled service users to negotiate with workers about what medication they needed and what they were prepared to take. Therefore, it is going to be more important than ever that social workers work with service users to try to form partnerships built on trust. However, it is going to be more difficult to do this, when there is a further imbalance of power created by Community Orders.

'Nearest relative'

The second change that the White Paper outlines is the change regarding 'nearest relative'. In the 1983 Mental Health Act, service users could not choose their nearest relative and sometimes, as in the case of Mrs Edwards, the nearest relative could be seen as acting against the best interests of the service user. The White Paper talks about 'nominated persons' and states that the service user may identify such a person in an advance agreement (Section 2.23). This is a very positive part of the Act, and will enable service users to have some control over who is involved in decisions regarding their mental illness.

Consent

The third change in the White Paper concerns service users who 'need treatment for serious mental disorder and are not able, because of long-term mental incapacity, to consent to care or treatment, although they do not resist it' (Section 6.3). It is interesting that the White Paper separates out this service user group. This, I believe, is a direct result of the Bournwood judgement referred to above. Unfortunately, although there are clearer safeguards in the White Paper than in the 1983 Mental Health Act, it does appear that these service users are to be treated differently from other service users. This may result in some service users (particularly those people with dementia and severe mental impairment) being moved into residential care. I think this can be seen from the case of Mrs Edwards who was originally in hospital at the time of the Bournwood judgement and this led to her being placed on a section, with Guardianship then being used to support her at home. If service users fall under this section of the new Act, they will receive a different service and there is no mention in the White Paper of compulsory powers in the community being available for this service user group. Instead it talks about working in the 'patient's best interests' and not with the patient (Section 6.9). It is going to be important that social workers argue for this service user group to receive the same opportunities to stay in the community as other service users.

Conclusion

This chapter has focused on Guardianship and the importance of building a relationship with a service user in order to empower her/him to take more control over her/his life. However, it has also shown that for some service users, it is important that legislation is used to provide a framework in which that relationship can take place. At present Guardianship does offer a real alternative to hospital for many service users. If the new Mental Health Act becomes law, it will be even more important for social workers to use legislative frameworks to promote good practice. As Braye and Preston-Shoot observe, 'If social work loses its ability or willingness to question and comment, it will lose its position to promote and empower a difference at the levels of both individual and collective experience' (1995, p.66). Social workers will have to utilise the legislation available as best they can to provide an empowering structure within which service users' needs can be met, so that once the Order is removed service users can continue to live successfully in the community with minimal state interference.

Notes

1   Applicable to England and Wales.

2   The term 'empowerment' is a very widely used term within social work practice. In this chapter it will be used to describe social work practice which has enabled service users who are often oppressed not only by society but also from within services to maintain some control over decisions regarding their own lives and in particular the treatment of their mental illness.

3   The functions given under the Act to approved social workers may only be carried out by officers of local social service authorities approved and appointed for this purpose (Department of Health 1999d, p.3).

4   The Butler Committee was set up to look at 'mentally abnormal offenders' and how this service user group was being maintained in the community. It stated that Guardianship could have a much wider role in maintaining in the community service users with mental illness and a forensic history.

5   Pseudonyms have been used for the two case studies.

6   Under the 1983 Mental Health Act (section 117), all patients who are detained under Section 3 have to have a planning meeting prior to their discharge which involves both health and social services. The meeting provides a care plan which will enable the person to return to the community. Any services that are to be provided as part of this care plan are to be paid for by health and social services and not the patient.

7   The Care Programme Approach was devised by the government in a document called *Building Bridges* (Department of Health 1995) which aimed to provide a seamless service to patients/service users. This means that health and social services have to work together, by jointly attending meetings and by completing joint paperwork.

8   The Bournwood case concerned 'L', who was a service user with severe learning difficulties. 'L' attended a day centre, and one day the driver of the bus to the day centre was changed and this caused 'L' to become distressed, so that by the time he reached the day centre he was displaying agitated behaviour. The professionals involved decided to place 'L' in hospital against his wishes and those of his carers. The carers took the case to court arguing that 'L' deserved the same rights regarding his detention in hospital as other service users with mental health problems. The outcome of the case was that 'L''s carers won. This led to widespread assessments of people in psychiatric hospitals, particularly those with dementia and learning difficulties. There was then an appeal which overturned the case. However, the effect of this case has been seen in that most service users with dementia and severe learning difficulties continue to be assessed under the Mental Health Act and thus have the same rights of appeal as other service users. The Bournwood case is awaiting possible appeal to the European Court of Human Rights.

over 85 years of age may have dementia. Of these, one third are expected to need constant care and attention (Audit Commission 2000).

In addition to greater awareness of mental health problems in later life, legislative developments underpinned and consolidated the establishment of our CMHT, especially the Mental Health Act (1983), with its expectation that health and social services departments would work more closely together with people experiencing mental health problems, and the community care reforms, culminating in the introduction of assessment and care management through the National Health Service and Community Care Act (1990).

The creation of a dedicated, multi-disciplinary, multi-agency community mental health team for older people offered clear advantages for service users. It cemented the commitment of health and social services, at a local level, to move away from institutional care, based on confinement and control, towards a more creative, community-based approach with an emphasis on self-determination and the promotion of lifestyles which are as independent as possible. A unified service, which reduced the need to deal with various separate agencies, was easier for service users to work with. Also indicated by the creation of a specialist team was the message that working with older people who have mental health problems was no longer considered a 'dead end', as in the traditional view (Marshall and Dixon 1996). Rather it was now seen as a worthwhile, challenging and rewarding field of practice, requiring specialist staff, resources and training.

It is clear that CMHTs for older people offer a practice setting in which multi-disciplinary partnerships can be advanced. The potential for such work has, however, often been bedevilled by debates and conflicts between the disciplines of nursing and social work contained within these teams. Such inter-professional divisions have been symbolised by and played out through respective professional attachment to the social model and the medical model of mental health. These conflicts all too easily become a sterile focus for professional mistrust. In contrast, we recognise and respect the utility of models and concepts in developing practice, but take the view that they are guiding means and not absolute truths. For example, take a hypothetical older person called John Smith. A social model may go some way towards explaining his perception of social redundancy in terms of an analysis of ageism. A medical model may lead to his hypertension being correctly diagnosed and treated. Genetics, biochemistry and other disciplines may offer further insights too. Each perspective can add something to our overall understanding of John, without needing to deny the validity of other approaches. However, our personal experience of John would tell us that he is much more than the sum total of all these analyses. Although each of them may have contributed a great deal to our understanding of him from their own particular but limited perspectives, reliance on conceptual knowledge of John alone would make it difficult to value him as an individual or recognise his individual needs.

This leads us to the view that dispute about models and concepts needs to be superseded by a shared commitment to moving forward with the determination to develop good practice through multi-disciplinary partnership. This orientation needs to be both practical and aimed at improving the quality of life of service users, rather than serving a sectarian professional agenda, and locally based, by which we mean tailored to the specific needs of a community. Above all, what is required is a person-centred practice, which requires us to avoid the temptation to reduce the complex lived realities of service users like our allegorical John Smith, as well as staff members, to a merely conceptual level but rather treats them as unique and valuable people. Ways of working which lead to the best outcomes for service users, not the promotion of the interests of a particular discipline, need to be the touchstone of multi-disciplinary partnership. This requires a willingness to trust each other and have good faith. Each team member should be committed to service users first, and not the advancement of the interests of their specific profession, because there is no room for cynicism in effective multi-disciplinary partnership. This means, for example, that discussions about developing a team's services need to be focused on the service user's interests and not on whether we can use this as an opportunity to swell the number of social workers in the team or get some more training for the health staff.

The precise forms practice based on multi-disciplinary partnership takes will be related to local and historical factors. For example, how health and social services are organised locally, their spending priorities, whether they are located in an urban or a rural area and local levels of poverty can all be expected to have an effect.

Principles for partnership

One of the ways of focusing multi-disciplinary partnership on the best outcomes for service users is to identify the negative practice features which can emerge and the positive principles to aim for.

The negative aspects revolve around limited professional visions, which tend to be manifested in fearfulness and a determination to pursue the nursing or social work project in isolation. It could be summarised in the statement, 'I will do my bit and you get on with what you lot do'. This leads to professional 'tribalism', which is characterised by splits along occupational lines. Such splits can take organisational and administrative forms. For example, the respective discipline meetings taking over the role of the multi-disciplinary team meeting, for the purposes of organising the business of the team unilaterally or developing parallel but separate case file recording. This can be reinforced by training and developmental activities being undertaken in separate camps. The result is fragmentation and this is inimical to the development of multi-disciplinary practice. Professional ideologies and mythologies, which are a feature of professional tribalism, sometimes lead to a tendency to deify a team member's own discipline while demonising others, with accompanying distrust and lack of mutual respect. In this context attempts can be made to intellectualise, rationalise and justify occupational sectarianism by resorting to models which, when misused in the service of sectarian projects, can be damaging to team relationships. The clearest example of this is crude attachment to the medical and social models as vehicles for maintaining destructive inter-professional relationships.

The positive principles which need to be asserted, as the basis from which the continuing challenges and dilemmas of multi-disciplinary partnership can be addressed, are:

- a firm belief in the value of moving forward together as an effective way of meeting the needs of service users

- appreciation of the need to develop practical, flexible means of working which are responsive to the changing needs of the local service user group

- acceptance of the benefits of working together in shared office accommodation, with streamlined administrative staff and systems, policies and procedures and common developmental activities

- active commitment by individual team members to the principle that multi-disciplinary practice requires the distinctive and complementary contributions of the different disciplines; this requires a thorough understanding and appreciation of each other's responsibilities, duties, knowledge, skills and value bases.

In the next section information is provided about the organisational and legal environment of the community mental health team for older people in which we work, as the context for the subsequent discussion of the issues and principles identified above.

The organisational context

The team in which we work was set up in 1985. Its brief from the outset was to support older people with both functional and organic mental health illnesses:

Organic and functional mental states

ORGANIC STATES

These are conditions where the organic structure of the brain has been affected by a disease process. The most common organically based conditions encountered by community mental health teams for older people are the dementias. Dementias involve progressive impairment of brain functioning. Symptoms include memory loss, disorientation, and deterioration of cognitive abilities. Hallucinations and challenging behaviour can also be symptoms of some forms of dementia. About 50 dementias have been identified. Alzheimer's disease accounts for about 60 per cent of diagnosed dementias and is characterised by a progressive decline in higher mental abilities leading to disintegration of intellect and personality. Strokes, tumours, neurological conditions and alcohol/substance abuse can also cause organically based mental illness.

FUNCTIONAL ILLNESSES

These have no discernible structural, organic cause but affect a person's mental health. For example:

- depression
- anxiety/phobic states
- paraphrenic disorder (a psychotic, paranoid state tending to affect older people where there is a fixed delusional system without general personality disintegration)
- schizophrenic illnesses
- bipolar disorders (a psychotic illness where there are mood swings, both manic and depressive)
- alcohol/substance abuse
- obsessive-compulsive disorder
- post-traumatic stress syndrome.

The aim of the team has been to assist service users to live as independently as possible, in their own homes whenever this can be achieved. It has sought to do this by assisting service users to achieve their optimum level of mental health and by attempting to reduce the damaging effects that discrimination based on mental health status can have for service users and significant others. We offer a case example of work with a service user later in the chapter to illustrate this aim.

The team serves a population of approximately 100,000 in a mixed urban and rural setting. At its inception, the team consisted of two community psychiatric nurses (CPNs). Following negotiations between the health trust and the social services department, its shift towards a multi-disciplinary orientation began in 1988 with the arrival of the first social work post. This signalled the beginning of steady, incremental development of the service. The team now comprises two social workers (employed by the social services department), four CPNs (employed by the NHS trust) and four community support workers (CSWs), three of whom are employed by health and one by social services, plus the team's own secretary. The team has access to the wider mental health services for older people in its operating area. These services include occupational therapy, an in-patient unit, a day hospital, a psychology department, psychiatrists, a counsellor for older people, a music therapist and an aromatherapist. The team is also able to use the range of social services available locally, for example, home care, day care, respite breaks and short-stay, residential and nursing placements, including specialist placements for older people with mental illnesses. In addition to the health services already mentioned, the team has access to two respite beds at a local non-acute hospital and respite beds purchased by the health trust in local residential homes.

The principal functions of the team are to assess the needs of and co-ordinate packages of care services for adults of any age with an organic mental illness and for adults over 70 years of age who have functional mental health illnesses. An open 'new referral' scheme is operated. Referrals come from prospective service users, carers, local social services adult teams, district nurses, general practitioners, the in-patient ward and other mental health service workers.

It is necessary for the agreement of the service user's GP to be forthcoming for a referral to be acted upon. This used to be partly because of GP fund-holding issues but is now more specifically due to the need to recognise and facilitate the GP role in collaborative mental health work. The team operates within a set of referral criteria, which have been agreed by the health trust and the social services department.

Referral to the community mental health team for older people

Principles

The main aim of the CMHT for older people is to provide, by means of a multi-disciplinary approach, a range of specialist mental health services for people of any age who have been diagnosed as having organic dementia and people of 70 years and above who have a functional mental illness.

The service will seek:

- to assist individuals to achieve their optimum level of mental health
- to reduce the damaging effects that mental health problems have upon individuals and their carers
- to support and sustain older people with mental health problems in the community, either in their own homes or in appropriate residential facilities.

Criteria for referring to the CMHT for older people

- Diagnosis of mental illness/dementia by a GP or consultant and a presenting mental health need as a result of it.
- Needs that cannot be met solely by other social work teams or any other agency/service.
- Before agreeing to take a case, initial assessment by a member of CMHT for older people will be carried out. Cases should not be closed/transferred until acceptance is confirmed.
- Good practice and continuity will determine continued involvement with a case, that is, joint working. Client needs will usually dictate this.
- CMHT for older people's capacity for urgent response is limited but is within CPA (Care Programme Approach) guidelines.
- Cases of disagreement will be referred to appropriate line managers.
- Guidelines/criteria to be reviewed six-monthly after implementation.

A team member will always be available to discuss suitability of referral or to offer advice.

Table 9.1 Workers' roles

Community psychiatric nurse	Community support workers	Social worker
Keyworker responsibilities	Rehabilitation	Keyworker responsibilities
Initial assessments	Motivating Clients	Initial assessments
Mental health assessments	Social support/assistance with re-socialisation	Holistic, needs-led assessments
Co-ordinating in-patient assessment	Contributions to assessment	Financial assessments
NVQ assessing/training in care work with CSWs	Support with activities of daily living	Care planning/management
S.117/CPA/after care responsibilities	Work in day-hospital and in-patient unit	Monitoring care package
Supervision of CSWs	Liaison with other agencies	Practice teaching/training
Input to locality planning	Updating case keyworker	S.117/CPA/after care responsibilities
Nursing/therapeutic input	Administration tasks and information technology	Supervision of CSWs
Access to health services	Support social worker or CPN in implementing delegated tasks	Input to locality planning
Administration and information technology		Benefits/welfare rights advice
Counselling		Access to social and health services
Liaison with other agencies		Administration and information technology
Monitoring health/medication		Facilitation of advocacy
Link role with all local residential and nursing homes		Liaison with other agencies

The team has never had a designated leader. Team management has come from a group comprising the line managers from the respective employing organisations and the respective first-line managers have supervised individual team members' work. CPNs and social workers have had responsibility for the supervision of community support workers employed by their respective agencies. This is typical of the way in which within its multi-disciplinary orientation the team has evolved a mix of roles and responsibilities. Some of these are shared and others are the preserve of specific occupational groups. (See Table 9.1.)

While separate responsibilities exist, there are commonalities too. An illustration of separate responsibilities is provided by CPNs' treatment and therapeutic input, social workers' involvement with care management and CSWs being engaged in 'hands-on' support and rehabilitation. Conversely, the most obvious common task of social workers, CPNs and CSWs is to contribute to the service user assessment process, albeit to different elements of that process. For example, a CPN's mental health assessment will tend to focus on issues of communication, orientation, cognitive abilities, memory and so on. Social work assessment will tend to consider needs associated with accommodation, access and transport, finances, mobility and self-care, as well as identifying and evaluating existing and potential sources of support (informal and from services), the needs of carers and the service user's personal biography and self-perceived needs. CSWs contribute information to assessments, based on regular close work with service users, about lifestyle preferences, routines, and other details, which assessments might have otherwise missed, but which are important to a service user's quality of life.

The team has regular, weekly meetings that alternate between a business and allocations format. At the allocations meeting, new referrals are discussed and work is allocated to the most appropriate professional(s). If workers from both disciplines are needed, a 'task agreement' is completed. This itemises the negotiated role of each professional. Should CSW input be needed, a 'delegated tasks agreement' is negotiated between the keyworker, be that a CPN or social worker, and the CSW, whose work on a particular case will be supervised by the keyworker.

In recognition of the different types of work required of team members, a rota system has evolved which separates out referrals already screened by initial assessment. A CPN or a social worker undertakes this initial assessment on a rota basis. It provides a succinct overview of the needs of a service user and risks presented by her/his current circumstances. This allows a decision to be made about whether the team should allocate the case and if so, which discipline(s) need to be involved. Alternatively, it forms the basis for other agency contact to be facilitated or appropriate advice to be given. CPNs have elected to use separate rotas to organise the other main elements of their work: initial assessments, mental health assessments, and after care (required by service users leaving in-patient wards), and a rota for co-ordinating in-patient assessments. Social workers chose to use one rota for their work, known as the 'care management rota'.

The legal context

Until now the Mental Health Act (1983) has been the pivotal piece of legislation governing the work of the whole team. However, the government is likely to introduce a new Mental Health Act. This follows publication of the White Paper, *Reforming the Mental Health Act* (Department of Health 2001a). We will consider some of the key provisions of the Mental Health Act 1983, as they affect our work and some of the other legislation relevant to our work with older people with mental health problems, before moving on to consider some of the proposed features of the new Act in the White Paper.

Service users fall into one or more of the categories of mental disorder identified by the Mental Health Act (1983) (i.e. mental illness, mental impairment, severe mental impairment or psychopathic disorder). They fit mainly into the mental illness category. A significant proportion of them will have come to the attention of the team following an in-patient admission. Some are informal patients but many have been detained under Section 2 of the Act, for assessment for up to 28 days and Section 3 for treatment (for up to six months initially and with the possibility of extension for another six months and then for 12-month periods). Emergency admissions under the terms of Section 4 of the Act have been infrequent.

In the case of Section 2 and Section 3 admissions, application will have been made by the approved social worker (ASW), as is usually the case, or the nearest relative (defined in order of seniority in Section 26 of the legislation and in practice a rare occurrence). The application will contain the recommendation of a doctor who knows the service user and another approved under Section 12 of the Act as a doctor competent to diagnose and treat mental disorder. The ASW is registered with the local authority in accordance with the provisions of the Act, following specialist mental health training, and his or her duties with respect to compulsory assessment and detention are covered by Section 13 of the Act.

The team is required, under the terms of Section 117 after-care arrangements (set out in the 1983 Act for patients being discharged from a Section 3 order), to assess service users' health and social needs, formulate an agreed care plan and allocate a keyworker to co-ordinate these tasks and implement monitoring and review arrangements. Reviews include service users and significant others and all those actively involved with the service user's care, such as the CPN, social worker and consultant psychiatrist. In addition, all service users over the age of 16 years who are leaving in-patient facilities and are receiving assistance from specialist mental health services are entitled to the Care Programme Approach (CPA). The Department of Health (1990b) makes this clear. Like Section 117, the CPA also requires systematic assessment of health and social needs for service users and monitoring and review arrangements involving all relevant parties, but this is less prescriptive than Section 117.

Team members are regularly involved in review tribunals and hospital managers' hearings, which are also derived from the Mental Health Act (1983). Review tribunals are established for each district by the Lord Chancellor and can consist of doctors, lay people and lawyers. Tribunals can hear appeals and listen to evidence about patients detained for more than six months under the provisions of Section 3. They can discharge patients from hospital, recommend leave from the hospital or supervised discharge, delay discharge or make conditional discharges. Workers in the team are sometimes asked to attend hospital managers' hearings, held for service users with whom they work. These are convened at the patient's request, on the renewal of detention under the Mental Health Act (1983) or where the nearest relative is barred from discharging the patient if this course is considered to pose unacceptable risk to the service user or others. Medical staff are in attendance so that all the workers involved with the service user can talk to the managers, the service user and significant others.

The social services department has received some of the service users we work with into Guardianship. (See Chapter Eight for a full discussion of Guardianship.) The team has been consistent in its interpretation of the law that Guardianship cannot be used solely to transfer a service user from hospital to residential care, against the service user's wishes.

Social workers in the team are often involved with the application of the Enduring Power of Attorney Act (1985). This enables the 'receiver' (usually a relative) to register an enduring power, which can be used in the event of the 'donor' (service user) becoming mentally incapacitated to the point where it is appropriate for another to manage their affairs and property. Applications are heard by a judge of the Court of Protection, a division of the Supreme Court, appointed by the Lord Chancellor. In some cases, social workers also become involved in giving advice, information and support to applicants to the Court of Protection for receivership. This is useful when a service user lacks sufficient mental capacity to manage her/his own affairs or to agree to enduring power of attorney arrangements, but nevertheless needs assistance from others. The Court can decide to accept responsibility for the service user's affairs and does this via a receiver, appointed by it to act in the service user's interests. The receiver would normally be a relative, a significant other or a solicitor. If there is nobody available who is suitable, the Official Solicitor may undertake this function. In addition to assistance with making initial applications to the Court of Protection, social workers routinely liaise with receivers regarding the welfare of the service user, for example, by initiating application by the receiver to the Court for the release of funds for a new heating system, if the service user's has broken down.

The primary focus of the White Paper, *Reforming the Mental Health Act* (Department of Health 2001a), appears to be the contention that care in the community, as presently organised, presents unacceptable dangers both to the public, in terms of the risk of homicides on the part of service users, and to the service users themselves in terms of suicides.

Part One of the White Paper deals with, among other topics, the perceived need to further develop powers of compulsory treatment of service users and how this might be done without falling foul of the Human Rights Act (1998). For example, the introduction of new independent tribunals to consider all longer-term use of compulsory powers is proposed, as is the right to an independent advocate for service users and a new mental health commission to keep the use of formal powers under review. These provisions, combined with the statutory use of individual care plans, are proposed to safeguard human rights.

For people deemed to need compulsory intervention from mental health services, the Mental Health Act (1983) sections are to be replaced by a three-stage assessment process. Stage One will commence based on the decision that further assessment/treatment is needed to avoid risk of serious harm to self or others following an initial assessment by two doctors and either a social worker or suitably trained health professional. It is interesting to note in this connection that the responsibilities previously residing with the approved social worker will now fall to any suitably qualified mental health worker. This may be a cause for concern as ASWs typically have a very good knowledge of community resources that sometimes enable the use of compulsory powers to be avoided. They are also trained to ensure the rights of the individual are upheld. It may be that other mental health professionals in community teams would, following suitable training, be able to undertake this function, thus creating greater flexibility and easing pressure of work on ASWs. However, the use of any 'suitably qualified person', including those working in in-patient units, would inevitably raise concerns that convenience may become more important than the independent assessment provided by an ASW or other mental health professional. In-patient staff may not be able to access or have knowledge of alternative resources in the community. This would seem to raise the possibility of service users' interests and rights becoming less important than operational convenience.

Stage Two involves a full assessment of health and social care needs, plus treatment as needed set out in a formal care plan, for up to 28 days on a compulsory basis. Further compulsory detention will be authorised by the new mental health tribunal. The new tribunal is envisaged as independent and will take advice from independent experts, the clinical team, service users and significant others. In Stage Three it can make a care and treatment order for a period of six months for the first two orders and twelve months for subsequent orders, in accordance with a care plan recommended by the clinical team. Unlike the current arrangements it is envisaged that these compulsory care and treatment orders will be applicable to patients living in the community as well as those in hospital settings. Although those living in the community cannot be subjected to forced medication, this will still be an option in clinical settings. The call for 'community treatment orders' in the community has been debated for many years (see, for example, Vernon 1990, p.183). However, the extension of compulsory powers has alarmed many who would welcome the increased support promised by the White Paper, such as the use of patient advocates and more investment, but are worried by the apparent coerciveness of its underlying outlook. A new organisation, the Mental Health Alliance, is campaigning against the extension of compulsory powers, under the slogan 'More Rights Less Wrongs', and includes the British Association of Social Workers, the British Psychological Society and the Critical Psychiatry Group among its members.

There are a number of positive features of the White Paper, first, the continued right to free legal representation of those subject to compulsory orders and a new right to independent advocacy and information about how the powers work in relation to their individual case. Second, the new act is likely to ensure the free exchange of information between agencies such as social services, health and housing services in an attempt to protect the health and safety of service users and others. Finally there is also a welcome promise in the White Paper that those who have long-term mental incapacity and are unable to give meaningful consent to treatment must be reviewed by the person with clinical responsibility. Another suitable clinician must provide a second opinion, since, as the White Paper recognises, this group is particularly at risk of abuse and neglect.

Social workers operate within a wide legislative framework and the principal pieces of legislation affecting their practice with service users, in addition to the legislation referred to above, are itemised in Table 9.2.

Table 9.2 Overview of legal framework
(not including Mental Health Act 1983)

1948 National Assistance Act: Includes a duty to provide residential placements to qualifying adults [S.21]; a general power to arrange community-based services for qualifying adults [S.29] and the power to arrange compulsory removal of qualifying adults at risk in specific circumstances from home to a place of safety [S.47]; a duty to protect the property of service users away from home in hospital, a care home, or a place of safety [S.48].

1968 Health Service and Public Health Act/1970 Chronically Sick and Disabled Persons Act: The Chronically Sick and Disabled Persons Act [S.2] did not specifically refer to older people, just chronically sick and disabled people. Government subsequently issued guidance to update the 1968 Health Service and Public Health Act to allow local authorities to provide such specific services as those in the 1970 Chronically Sick and Disabled Persons Act to older people specifically. Since the 1968 Act already contained a general clause about promoting the needs of older people under S.45, this was a convenient way of extending the right to such specific services to older people.

1976 Race Relations Act: Contains a duty for local authorities to provide appropriate services to different ethnic groups on the basis of equity [S.71].

1977 National Health Service Act: Explicitly requires the provision of home care and help to those assessed as needing it. [Sch.8]

1990 National Health Service and Community Care Act: Contains a duty to assess needs and arrange services to meet identified needs of adults [S.47].

1995 Carers (Recognition and Services) Act: Contains a duty to assess the needs of carers providing regular and substantial care and to take them into account when planning services for users.

In the next section we will identify the main issues the team has faced in terms of multi-disciplinary partnership and the attempts which have been made to address problems constructively.

Identification of multi-disciplinary partnership issues

Putting staff with different professional backgrounds and different employing organisations together in a team has, in our experience, raised a number of problems. These problems tend to equate with the negative aspects introduced earlier in the chapter. Most people joining the team have a strong commitment to the service user group *and* their own profession. They also have a familiarity with the way in which their employing organisation usually operates in terms of policy and procedure. Few, however, have worked in a multi-disciplinary team before and so there is usually little comprehension of the role and value of other disciplines. Multi-disciplinary policies, procedures, customs and practice can be confusing because they contain elements of the familiar but also much that was previously unknown. This can be disempowering for new team members and has meant that many of us have struggled initially to identify with the team. There has been a tendency to 'stick with what I know' (a limited professional vision), and redouble belief in the value of one's own background to the exclusion of effective joint work. This represents a lack of trust in the competence or relevance of other disciplines and cynicism about the value of multi-disciplinary partnership. Unnecessary duplication of assessment work, with workers from both nursing and social work backgrounds asking a service user similar questions, is an example of this limited professional vision and stems from an assumption that the other worker is not so well equipped to procure the necessary information. This can waste time and also reduce the service user's confidence in the professionalism and advantages of the multi-disciplinary team.

Lack of confidence in other disciplines' assessment skills can lead to rivalry and jealousy within the team. It has meant that many new staff members have found their early experience of the team very difficult. Team members have come to realise that special attention needs to be paid to the specific induction needs of new staff joining multi-disciplinary teams in order to enable them to develop their confidence so that they are able to accept support from and give good quality advice to colleagues from different professional backgrounds. The team's practice now reflects the understanding that induction needs to include the value of a multi-disciplinary team to the service user, the value and distinctive contributions of the various disciplines, information about the team's policies, procedures, customs and practices, its historical development, expectations of team members and team decision-making processes and accountability. Although we have observed issues arising from limited professional vision being particularly visible when one first begins multi-disciplinary practice, we do not wish to imply that it is no longer a danger to established team members from all occupational backgrounds. Regular team-building activities are an essential corrective to this tendency and need to include both staff and their managers from both the local NHS Health Trust and the local authority social services department. Activities can focus on regular professional updates from acknowledged authorities in the field, information-sharing between both agencies on forthcoming developments likely to affect the team, question-and-answer sessions between staff and managers and analysis of joint learning and developmental needs.

Professional 'tribalism' (by which we mean organisational, administrative and developmental splits, such as professional development activities in the team carried out along occupational lines) has been a destructive feature of our work together at times. It has often been exacerbated by external factors. For example, the team's original 'single case file' approach, with all workers sharing a common case file, had clear advantages in terms of shared access to information. It has been undermined by the introduction of new, and thus far incompatible, information technology systems by the respective employers. Social workers now record exclusively on the social services system which is inaccessible to other staff. The community care reforms, as a consequence of the implementation of the National Health Service and Community Care Act (1990), have also had a significant impact. The emphasis placed on comprehensive, holistic, needs-led assessment, combined with ongoing care planning, monitoring and review responsibilities, although welcomed as measures likely to improve our service to service users, significantly increased the workload of social workers. They were simultaneously required to pay more attention to financial assessments and to assisting with the completion of benefits forms and the recording of care package costing details. Cases tended to need to stay open to social workers for longer periods, post assessment, for the monitoring and review of expensive resources and social workers who had originally served on the initial assessment rota alongside CPNs had to reduce that commitment. A further external factor, which has sparked off episodes of professional 'tribalism', is limited resources. In this context, it is all too easy to slip into a 'blame culture' in which specific agencies are regarded as at fault and their motives are questioned. While the Care Programme Approach has a health lead, care management lead rests with social services whose staff have responsibility to 'gatekeep' social care services for which their local authority is financially responsible. CPNs have therefore been increasingly prevented from accessing social care services for their clients directly.

These experiences of tendencies towards professional 'tribalism' have convinced team members of the importance, at every level, of a long-term commitment on the part of both services to multi-disciplinary partnership. Transparent decision-making processes and visible measures, on the part of managers from both organisations, demonstrate their ongoing interest and commitment to the team. Importance is attached to anticipating and planning for changes, as far ahead as possible, analysing their likely impacts and regularly monitoring and reviewing team functioning. The absence of this ongoing commitment to a joint approach to problem-solving would, in our view, make a slip back into 'tribalism' more likely.

However, although professional 'tribalism' has often been exacerbated by external factors, we believe it is fuelled by something more fundamental, namely, professional ideologies and mythologies. From the perspective of CPNs, enduring mythologies are that social workers produce intuitive assessments without reference to hard data and are primarily interested in budgets and resources. Care management is 'just gatekeeping' and a matter of 'filling in a few forms' which anybody could do. Despite this, social workers 'have their uses' but 'they don't work as hard as we do'. Social work myths include seeing CPNs as overprotective and opposed to service users taking risks, as assessing the condition rather than the person's individual needs, as being unable to complete holistic assessments and as being profligate with resources. They, too, 'have their uses' but 'they don't work as hard as we do'.

These myths are damaging. They are inimical to joint work and underpin professional tribalism and limited professional visions. The myths can, in our experience, usually be traced to bad experiences with members of different disciplines, to the prejudices of colleagues, to insecurity at a personal level and to the status of a discipline in the team, as well as its national fortunes. The demise of myths is hastened by exposure to complementary disciplines in a multi-disciplinary setting. We hope that in the case study, presented later in the chapter, we have demonstrated that CPNs, for example, are involved in risk assessment and management to enable service users to continue living independently. Also, that social workers can collect and evaluate hard data and deploy an understanding of mental health, as well as contribute to the formulation of creative care packages, which are not simply the result of financial calculation. Such practice experiences have helped us to counter among ourselves the destructive power of ideologies that have followed members of different disciplines through their careers from basic training onwards.

The social model versus the medical model of mental health is central. Social workers tend to be trained in terms of the validity of the social model and the medical model is viewed with suspicion, mainly because it is seen as oppressive. They may enter practice with the view that the social model is person-centred, focuses on need as a consequence of social, cultural, structural and environmental discrimination against the service user group, and emphasises the civil rights of service users. The medical model is seen, on the other hand, as focusing on the condition, not the person, on care-giving rather than enablement, on functional 'deficits' instead of abilities and on care and control rather than empowerment. From a nursing perspective, it is seen as essential to focus on diagnosis, treatment, care and rehabilitation in order to enhance quality of life. A focus on social issues may be viewed as laudable but also as peripheral to the central issues at hand. It does not aid diagnosis, treatment or care-giving and can be a screen for avoidance of hard decision-making, introducing altogether too much politics and insufficient practical reality.

In our experience working in the team, these positions are entrenched and inform much professional strife. We find this ironic because our reflection together on the issues raised has led us to the conclusion that these positions are symbolic rather than real. Their tenacity seems to be linked to their 'sacred' nature in the respective discipline's perspectives. They are not, however, linked to our experience of what actually happens in practice, where we believe that pragmatism tends to hold sway. The reality of multi-disciplinary practice is that the value of both perspectives is appreciated as a necessary feature of best practice. Accordingly, we think that multi-disciplinary partnership is an ideal environment in which best practice can flourish. Team multi-disciplinary assessments are holistic and include consideration of both medical and social factors impacting on life chances. They are needs-led, not model-led, and emphasis is placed on the individual needs, views, preferences and biography of the service user, not resources or medical condition. There is what we consider to be a realistic understanding that service users' difficulties arise from a complex of factors, deriving from social origins and medical status.

Members of the team share a commitment to a number of values, which underpin good practice. We are committed to independent living solutions and this, as we have seen earlier, was a founding principle. Recently, this has included looking at ways of supporting service users in sheltered housing complexes as an alternative to residential care. The team has a good record of service user advocacy too, which the case study will illustrate. There is a strong emphasis placed on inclusive practice (i.e. using the assessment process to encourage individual service users to identify needs relating to their social location, based on factors such as ethnicity, gender and disability). This is in order to avoid imposing an ideological interpretation of such needs, which can sometimes be a feature of anti-discriminatory practice. We see the value of such an approach as located in its tendency to place the service user 'centre-stage' and work towards a solution which takes into account her/his experience of discrimination.

It stands in contrast to many approaches to 'anti-discriminatory practice', which appear to start with an ideology, rather than the service user, 'centre-stage', move to a solution based on the ideology and then apply this to the individual service user's situation. Such an approach is questionable in our judgement, since it can disempower service users by imposing our world view on their lived reality. This mirrors the old service-led rather than needs-led approach to service provision, albeit from a supposedly more 'progressive' political perspective. Workers go to considerable lengths to engage service users in the assessment process and this has included consideration of communication issues and issues concerning 'challenging' behaviour and its interpretation.

Perhaps a useful corrective to the entrenched medical model versus social model debates of the past is to begin consciously to reckon the benefits of multi-disciplinary partnership in advancing best practice ideals. A useful starting point might be to introduce shared units of basic professional training for CPNs and social workers and make knowledge and skills in and of multi-disciplinary working an essential part of the curricula for both disciplines. Practical measures, to be discussed next, have helped us to tackle some symptoms of professional ideology but this is just scratching the surface.

Addressing the issues raised by multi-disciplinary partnership

During the history of our multi-disciplinary team, managers and staff from both health and social services have committed time and energy to initiatives, which have attempted to develop the team in a positive direction and improve our work together. Those we consider to have been especially useful are described below.

First, the keyworker role has been a central aspect of developing the team's practice. As defined locally, the keyworker has the responsibility for co-ordinating assessment and care planning activity, providing information to service users about assistance available, liaising with services, maintaining regular contact with service users and undertaking monitoring and reviews. Perhaps the most important message this sends is that work has become more focused, through systematic multi-disciplinary assessment, on the individual and her/his needs, abilities, preferences, personal history and interests, rather than just on 'the disease' and its progression. Crucially, it gives clear overall responsibility for co-ordinating multi-disciplinary inputs to one person from either a social work or CPN background, via negotiation based on the nature of the service user's needs. This means that the user's needs are placed centre-stage and that the value of both disciplines is recognised.

Second, beginning in the mid-1990s, 'away days' (these are days away from the office and normal duties where the team can concentrate on building itself up without distractions) have assisted the members of the team to develop a firm belief in the value of working together as the best means of meeting the needs of the service user group. In our opinion such exercises are of great value and need to be a regular feature of team life.

Third, values clarification exercises have assisted the team to share an active commitment to good practice. We have established joint written principles which include putting the service users' and the carers' needs first, being clear about respective roles and affirming the value of our work together. A focus on role clarification has assisted this process and helped workers to appreciate the contributions of the different disciplines.

Fourth, an agreed referral protocol, rota system and task agreements between social workers and CPNs, as well as delegated task agreements between keyworkers and CSWs, have all assisted the team to further its aim of developing practical means of working which are responsive to service users and which discourage professional tribalism.

Fifth, regular team meetings, which alternate with the allocation meeting, have also been a positive development. The bi-weekly format allows workers to get away from the constant round of case allocation and discuss issues of mutual professional interest, as well as training and development opportunities. These meetings have been most helpful in building team identity. Of particular significance is the increasing tendency towards joint training for CPNs, CSWs and social workers. A very significant package of training courses was introduced. This included an intensive four-day course about dementia. With a strongly person-centred emphasis on the latest developments in anti-oppressive practice for work with older people with dementia, it set the scene for additional single-day sessions on particular issues, for example, advocacy and sexuality. This development, more than any other, assisted the team to begin to see that good practice needed to go beyond an artificial split between a supposed social model and medical model duality.

Sixth, the jewel in the crown in terms of promoting the value of flexible, joint work and an active commitment to it has been locality planning. This involves regular meetings between workers and managers to evaluate progress and to plan for the future. These meetings have not always been easy. On the contrary, sometimes they have either been quite challenging or have felt like a 'rubber stamping' exercise. However, when the dynamics have been right, locality planning has been an excellent means of affirming the team and its project. The format taken has been that individual team members have agreed to contribute and present specific material of interest to them, for example, statistics about our service user populations, service take-up, referral rates and sources, recent service developments, possible future developments. Presentations are made and are followed by managers engaging with team members about their proposals, as well as introducing their own. Constructive criticism is also forthcoming and it is a feature of the growing confidence of the team that this can now be accepted relatively well.

All the features of our team life described in this section have helped but we feel we cannot reiterate often enough the need for a consistent will on the part of workers and managers to use them on an ongoing basis. To illustrate progress that we feel has been made we turn to a case study which has involved social workers, CPNs and CSWs. This case study demonstrates how our multi-disciplinary partnership can be effective.

'Peter'

Peter, an older man living at home, initially attracted attention because of concerns expressed by the police. Following an in-patient admission, he wished to remain living at home. Peter was upset by various incidents in which he had been removed from shops, a local school and a train, sometimes with police involvement. Some local people found him frightening and felt he should be 'put away'. This was also the view of some members of the police and a number of parents of children at the school. Psychiatric and psychological intervention indicated a likely dementia and that Peter might have some degree of autism.

The assessment process involved a social worker, a CPN, and a CSW. The social worker spent time with Peter over the course of several visits in order to discover how he perceived his situation and his needs. What emerged was that Peter was proud of his career as a skilled worker but since retirement on health grounds had developed a lifestyle which he enjoyed, although not as much as he would like because he had less money. He had a very strict and inflexible routine from which he drew strength. This involved eating identical meals each day at the same times, a particular shopping routine, regular walks over several established routes, watching videos about natural history and geography in the evenings and writing out recipes from a book at regular intervals each day, to replace work as a draughtsman. Peter, a very private man, disliked anybody interfering in his life and did not understand why his interest in waving at young schoolchildren, stealing the things he needed and tapping out tunes on restaurant tables were a problem.

We negotiated the need for a formal assessment process and care planning in order to attempt to fulfil Peter's wishes and tackle the issues of concern to others. The assessment process examined issues of accommodation, health, (mental and physical), activities of daily living, finances, informal support, service network, personal biography, personal views about needs, and risks posed to and by Peter; it concluded that in order to support Peter to remain living independently, as he wished, a number of things needed to happen.

First, the social worker needed to handle accumulating debts, and liaised with creditors, the service user and his family to resolve this issue and to monitor progress.

Second, it was important to assess risk to children. Internal checks were made within the social services department and lateral checks were made by the social worker. These are checks made with other organisations involved in child protection, such as the police. Nothing suspicious was indicated. It was considered significant that Peter only seemed to appear at the school when parents were there at opening and closing times and he seemed to have no interest in any particular child. Rather, he waved at the children and greeted them *en masse*. This issue was resolved by team members, social worker and CPN, discussing with the head of the school the concerns of the parents, children and staff and our evaluation of the negligible risks posed, and coming to an agreement that Peter would be accompanied by staff from the team at the critical school times as a confidence-building measure. It was felt that this option presented the least coercive course of action, involving little curtailment of Peter's lifestyle. Other advantages were believed to be that parents and children would be encouraged to adopt an attitude less based on fear of people with mental health problems.

Third, it became clear that Peter was being victimised by shops and a train company because of unconventional, but harmless, behaviour. It was agreed, in liaison with the CSW, that more tolerant alternative services would be accessed in the case of shops and that representations would be made by the social worker to shops and the train company which appeared to have used discriminatory language and actions. This proved successful and Peter ended up with some monetary compensation from the train company which, like one of the shops, pledged to review staff training too.

Fourth, it was arranged that Peter would be referred to a consultant psychiatrist to attempt to establish the disease process. Two possibilities had emerged: frontal lobe dementia and Asperger's syndrome. A conclusive diagnosis might help to improve Peter's quality of life by suggesting an appropriate drug regime, behavioural intervention, therapies or social skills training.

Fifth, Peter has received a regular weekly visit from the CSW to assist him in pursuing his interests safely, for example driving out which Peter can no longer do since his driving licence was revoked, and assisting him in socially awkward situations, since he has tended to be a recipient of abuse from some local people. The CSW and Peter built a strong professional relationship which produced valuable insights into Peter's preferences. Further roles of the CSW were to assist with food hygiene, an area of concern, and to help Peter to remember to make arrangements to attend a regular clinic (he has a prosthesis), so that his mobility would not be adversely affected. Peter was also helped to plan the purchase of essential clothing.

All of this work was undertaken in a manner which fully involved Peter, who was encouraged to state his preferences. It enabled him to remain living at home, independently and relatively safely. It aimed to ensure that the effects of discrimination were minimised. It was understood, however, that psychiatric diagnosis and treatment were likely to be essential factors in establishing the cause of Peter's difficulties and considering whether drug therapy could assist him. The CPN's knowledge of the two conditions which it was felt might be affecting Peter's behaviour contributed to confidence-building measures with the community. In our view this kind of co-operative, multi-disciplinary work provides an impetus to move beyond petty organisational and ideological limitations.

Overall co-ordination was provided by the social worker (keyworker) with support from the CPN. The CPN was actively involved in the holistic assessment process, as well as advocacy on behalf of Peter, and contributed to the initiative to maintain him as independently as possible in the community according to his wishes. The social worker was able to contribute to the process in terms of the investigation into any previous offending behaviour against children and a needs-led approach to meeting needs.

Peter was enabled to pursue his wish to remain living independently, with minimum supervision and interference from others. This case study demonstrates that the social–medical model duality has little to offer 'real life' multi-disciplinary partnership practice.

Conclusion

We believe the case for multi-disciplinary partnership, as an effective means of meeting the needs of older people with mental health problems, is clear and resonates with the priorities and values set down recently by the Audit Commission (Audit Commission 2000). In many ways local developments have anticipated and proactively responded to needs, for example, through the team's commitment to effective multi-disciplinary assessment and appropriate, flexible and responsive 'joined-up' services arranged by health and social services and available to service users who live at home in the community. However, we hope our account has made it clear that the process may not be easy or painless at 'grass-roots' level. The process of change in our team proved challenging but the strong flexible systems described, which have been regularly reviewed and revised at locality planning meetings, have enabled progress to be made.

For service users and carers advantages have included a dedicated service, rationalised service provision, a specialist staff group committed to this particular area of work, a seamless, 'one-stop' service, with one keyworker co-ordinating the service but with access to many sources of assistance, and the benefits of a multi-disciplinary perspective. Staff have gained the opportunity to pursue a specialised field of interest with the advantages that this brings in terms of dedicated facilities, focused training, committed colleagues and opportunities to shape service delivery.

However, there are areas of weakness too, which frustrate multi-disciplinary partnership. These are based on different professional cultures and interests, divergent information technology and other systems, varying organisational priorities and agendas between the employers and the tenacity of professional and organisational ideologies, often masquerading as opposed models of practice. Despite this, experience in the team has shown that a consistent and united effort to overcome difficulties can produce considerable progress.

The current status of the multi-disciplinary team can be viewed as being transitional. It is not fully integrated but has taken the first steps away from professional separatism with all the disadvantages that this redundant vision has created in the past, such as professional and organisational rivalry, unco-ordinated services, a plethora of entry points into a disconnected system of service delivery and little in the way of specialist staff. In our view the current national political environment is favourable to the continuing evolution of multi-disciplinary partnership, given the emphasis placed by the government on joined-up work and seamless services. *Modernising Social Services* (Department of Health 1998a) and *Partnership in Action* (Department of Health 1998b) underlined the government's commitment to closer work between health and social services and led to extensive consultation. Removal of legal obstacles to pooled budgets and the promotion of joint investment plans and integrated service provision, with financial incentives for both health and social services, are a feature of Chapter 7 of *The NHS Plan* (Department of Health 2000a), as is the proposal to establish joint care trusts to be responsible for commissioning health and social services. *The NHS Plan* also proposes that multi-disciplinary community mental health teams will be the norm in the provision of community-based services for service users with mental health problems.

We welcome these developments in what we see as an inevitable process of unification of health and social services in the provision of care to our service users. They have been mirrored by initiatives by our local health and social service authorities to develop better mental health services on a countywide basis for older people. These have included agreement about a joint development plan in 1996, extensively reviewed by stakeholders in 1999/2000, and an extensive consultation exercise with service users, managers and independent service providers in 2000/2001 about the next steps. However, we are also strongly of the opinion, based on our experience of work in the team, that the proposed harmonisation of organisations and resources, envisaged in current policy must be accompanied by extensive consultation with staff and service users on the part of health and social services authorities in localities, as well as with the professional bodies, such as the British Association of Social Workers and, the Royal College of Nursing.

Also needed will be joint, multi-professional training aimed at developing the specific knowledge, skills and values needed in order to be a competent professional worker in a multi-disciplinary community mental health team. Such training, which we would see as additional to basic professional training in one of the constituent disciplines, would do much to overcome the difficulties associated with professional mythologies and ideologies. This ties in with the wider issue of the need for those responsible for the education of social workers and health professionals to look carefully at their own role in promoting less insular and exclusive approaches to health and social care. This might result, for example, in some joint practice placement provision and student assessment as well as the development of new models of multi-disciplinary practice.

While the opportunities afforded by the current political climate would appear to be favourable to those wishing to aid the continuing development of high quality services through multi-disciplinary community mental health teams, the work to be done would appear to be considerable. It will require much new thinking. We do not expect that there will be an overnight transformation of services but we hope we will see sustained, incremental advances in multi-disciplinary partnership.

Chapter Ten

Developing Good Practice
Prospects and Possibilities

Chris Hallett

Introduction

The book began by reviewing the implications for social work of the gale of change which has blown through community care in recent years (see Chapter One). One of the certainties for the future is that there is further change on the horizon for social work and community care. In facing more change, social services are relevant to all people who are unable to meet their own social welfare needs, particularly those who are most disadvantaged and vulnerable. The latter are under increasing pressure. National data on income and wealth shows that since 1979, the richest 10 per cent have become 62 per cent richer, while the poorest 20 per cent are no better off (Mason 1997, p.1). As an acknowledgement of the fact that life has become much more difficult for such people in recent years, Warwickshire County Council has produced a community development strategy, with emphasis on the most disadvantaged areas of the county. In addition to increasing disadvantage, there are social and demographic changes taking place. The number of people aged over 85 years old will rise by 50 per cent in the next 15 years; there are a growing number of people with learning disabilities living in the community; and people are being cared for in their own homes for longer, with any hospital admission being of short duration (Mason 1997, p.1). In this context, most of the support needed falls within the community care field. The concept of partnership, which has run throughout the contributions to this book, will remain crucial to the services provided, both in terms of agencies working together and by further participation in decision-making by service users and their carers.

Change... and more change

In facing further changes on the community care horizon, there is much to provide encouragement in terms of how change has been tackled thus far. The amount of change initiated by legislation and central government policy built up to a furious pace across the closing years of the twentieth century, often leaving front-line managers and social workers reeling from the lack of time for consolidation or for taking stock. Despite the pressures inherent in managing a mind-blowing volume of change, practitioners have demonstrated remarkable flexibility and adaptability, especially in respect of the development of partnership in user-centred services and in collaborative working with other agencies. Examples of this type of adaptability and flexibility are given by Walters (Chapter Five) in her account of partnership in a community setting as constituting the basis for a multi-agency care scheme facilitated by social services, health and an independent provider, and in the move from collaboration to partnership described by Roy and Watts (Chapter Four) which has occurred in a hospital setting. Perhaps it is not surprising that social work has been able to respond in such effective ways, given that the very nature of social work practice lies in seeking to achieve changes in circumstances for service users and their carers. Effective as social workers have been in adapting to change in the recent past, they will need all of their capabilities and resilience to continue to adapt in the future.

In part this is because changes within social work and community care have been implemented against a backcloth of increased expectations. Service user movements, such as disability groups, have become particularly effective in lobbying and campaigning and some of the national voluntary organisations are probably more prominent than at any time in their history. Add to this the fact that more service users and carers are challenging social workers' individual decisions, and in some cases are seeking legal redress, and a scenario emerges in which social work needs to be rigorous, accessible and accountable in order to sustain its future credibility. Morrison (Chapter Two) provides an excellent example of moving practice in written assessments with service users in just such a direction.

Adaptability and resilience will also be needed as the settings in which rigorous, accessible and accountable practice is being developed continue to be reconstituted in the early years of the twenty-first century, particularly at the interface of health and social services. For example, the boundary between community nursing and home care services has changed significantly. Not many years ago, home helps predominantly did housework and the bath nurse called to provide personal care. Over a relatively short space of time, home helps have moved to a situation in which they do hardly any housework and the vast majority of their tasks involve personal care of service users. As Tanner shows (Chapter Seven), the community care reforms promoted such shifts. A further example is provided by the increase in the number of people now provided with services in their own homes, in part as a consequence of the number of hospital beds having been reduced with some hospitals having closed and also as a result of a great deal of energy having been put into effecting speedy hospital discharges in order to reduce 'bed-blocking'. There has been an accompanying rise in the number of residential and nursing home placements, despite the recent closure of some homes, and the overall effect has been a substantial increase in accommodation provided outside the hospital setting, primarily funded by social services and/or service users and their relatives.

These major changes have forced social services departments to prioritise because there are insufficient resources to meet the needs of a growing number of service users, especially older people, living in the community. By narrowing the criteria for providing services, the services have been targeted at those in greatest need. The tensions created by moving tasks and responsibilities from health to social services have led to the realisation that neither health nor social services on their own can provide the type and quality of services which service users and their carers will expect in the future. Thus, many initiatives in recent years have been about moving health and social services closer together in terms of strategy, planning and service delivery. The chapters by Roy and Watts (Chapter Four), Walters (Chapter Five) and Millen and Wallman-Durrant (Chapter Nine) are indicative of the impact of initiatives so far. Primary care groups provide another example of closer joint working. They are being moved towards trust status and, once they have become care trusts, will be able to encompass tasks currently undertaken by social services departments.

To what extent are the developments outlined above an opportunity or a threat for social work and community care? What are the prospects and possibilities?

Prospects

The image and standing of social work in public perception has for many years been at a low level, with negative media coverage and a string of enquiries into poor practice. If there was ever a need rapidly to turn this around, then now is the time. Much hope for a boost in the image and standing of social work is enshrined in the new General Social Care Council. For the first time, it provides a platform for a strong and inclusive professional body independent of social services departments. For a number of years, the Association of Directors of Social Services has been the main representative of the social work profession. While this group has tried valiantly to fill the void caused by the absence of a strong professional body, it has lacked the quality of independence because it has been associated with protecting or securing resources for social services departments.

The General Social Care Council is likely to regulate social work in very different contexts to that of the near monopoly position occupied until fairly recently by social services departments. The driving of the health agenda, with primary care groups becoming trusts and then possibly care trusts as previously noted, means that the delivery of community care services for adults is ripe for change. This could leave children's services within social services, linked to changes within the local education authorities, as more schools have decentralised budgets and their own more powerful governing bodies. The decreasing central role for the local education authority might then revolve around special educational needs. Does this scenario herald a split in the bases for service provision, with the retention in local government of a restructured children's service and adult services hived off to health? Probably not, as examination of *The NHS Plan* (Department of Health 2000a) reveals that while the future development of care trusts would combine the provision of health and social care by one provider, the commissioning and scrutiny roles would be retained by the local authority. All of this suggests that while the direct provision of services may very well be delivered from within care trusts, a very important function of quality assurance would still be within a local government setting.

How are these possible changes likely to affect social work? As I indicated earlier, social work has a history of flexibility and adaptability in managing change. It has also been a champion of service user involvement and empowerment, anti-oppressive practice and the social model of disability. Through care in the community it has assisted thousands of people to move out of institutionalised hospitals. It has often worked with situations and people, whereas others might have walked away. However, a new dimension in social work's changing environment is competition from other professionals to take on work previously undertaken by social workers: 'Nurses and social workers may be increasingly in competition for the same territory, with nurses moving into counselling, care management and community liaison' (McLeod and Bywaters 2000, p.107). In response to this competition, social work will need to change again. There is evidence that these changes are already happening, for example, there are rapid response teams being introduced to prevent hospital admissions or to discharge people more quickly back to their own homes (see Chapters Four and Five). Millen and Wallman-Durrant in their account of multi-disciplinary work in a community mental health team (Chapter Nine) produce a table comparing the workers' roles within that team (see p.156). It is apparent from this table that there is a great similarity between the social worker and community psychiatric nurse roles. When changes are brought into force via proposed new mental health legislation, which removes the ring-fenced statutory role for approved social workers and enables health professionals to take on these tasks, the roles will become blurred even further (see Barry's discussion in Chapter Eight).

It is perhaps a little simplistic to rely only on lists of tasks for particular occupational roles and, accordingly, Millen and Wallman-Durrant (Chapter Nine) go on to identify the manner in which different professionals approach their role:

> The social model versus the medical model of mental health is central. Social workers tend to be trained in terms of the validity of the social model and the medical model is viewed with suspicion, mainly because it is seen as oppressive. They may enter practice with the view that the social model is person-centred, focuses on need as a consequence of social, cultural, structural and environmental discrimination against the service user group, and emphasises the civil rights of service users. The medical model is seen, on the other hand, as focusing on the condition, not the person, on care-giving rather than enablement, on functional 'deficits' instead of abilities and on care and control rather than empowerment. (p.165)

While Millen and Wallman-Durrant emphasise that this is only one contribution to multi-disciplinary teamwork, it is nevertheless an important aspect. It points to the significance of holding on to the value base of social work in the closer collaborative relationships between different professionals and agencies, which will become an increasingly common experience for social workers, as the contributions to this book make clear.

Roy and Watts (Chapter Four) provide an account of moving from collaboration to partnership in a hospital setting, with an account of four jointly planned projects. Collaboration implies the coming together of people to agree a planned action, while still retaining their individual identity. This is a feature in a number of projects described in this book. So is this different from partnership? Roy and Watts argue that it is and that there is a need for a shift from collaboration to partnership in the future. Their view concurs with the modernisation proposals for both health and social services, which map out a ten-year programme of investment and reform to reshape services (Department of Health 1998a, 2000a). Partnership is seen as the parties having greater shared ownership of the process and outcomes in the delivery of a seamless service. Partnership is portrayed as a step on from collaboration.

Lalani and Whiting (Chapter Three) take this concept of partnership into a different context. They analyse their work with minority ethnic communities in terms of their adherence to a model of partnership and user participation. They also identify the challenges of managing imbalances of power in this model and show how complex and time-consuming this can be in practice:

> By partnership, we mean engaging with, and encouraging the participation of, the Black communities in the planning, development and delivery of services to meet their needs, in a way that had not been tried with the majority white community up to that point. (pp.51–52)

They identify three important dimensions of the model of partnership:

- managing imbalances of power
- clear and strong leadership
- political support.

Despite the complexity involved in practising effective partnership, it is one of the key prospects for the survival of social work. Social work may not be able to be a stand-alone service in the future but it can make a valuable contribution, along with other professionals, to achieving changes in service users' circumstances.

The opportunity to develop a partnership model will exist within the framework for the implementation of the NHS Plan (Department of Health 2001b) and the changes it will bring for community care. The implementation plan sets out the framework within which regional and local plans will fit. It provides the framework for reviewing Health Improvement Plans and agreeing Service and Financial Frameworks, Joint Investment Plans (JIPs) and Primary Care Investment Plans (PCIPs). The NHS Plan is a radical development that involves both reform and future investment in services. In order to take this forward it is a requirement that each health authority establishes a 'Modernisation Board', which will involve front-line staff, local councils and other key partners to advise and oversee the implementation locally. Social services will be represented on these boards, thus providing an opportunity to influence future planning.

In considering partnership as a key to social work's prospects, I have been concerned in the main with the impact of change on social work. However, there is a key element of social work which we should seek to hold on to proactively in the midst of change, namely participation in both the design and delivery of services by service users and carers. Participation has grown steadily in importance over the years and is a distinctive feature of social services' contribution to community care. Tanner (Chapter Seven) points to the resourcefulness of older people in a way which suggests their potential as participants, rather than passive subjects:

> The study has shown that older people are immensely resourceful in the strategies they use to try to manage their difficulties and that for the most part they are knowledgeable about their specific needs and the help they require to address them... The key message from this for assessors and service providers is to treat people as experts in their own problem-solving and to seek to build on their existing strengths and strategies. (p.126).

The notion that service users are the experts, and that they should be empowered to contribute as much as possible to decision-making and the design of their care packages, is much more prevalent in social work than elsewhere. As partnership between professionals becomes more common, this emphasis on participation will add value to overall service delivery.

Fleming and McSparran (Chapter Six) take a close look at empowerment as a participative process and ask the question, 'Are social work and occupational therapy seen as empowering by service users and carers?' By drawing on Dalrymple and Burke's model of empowerment, they find that there is still much progress to be made in achieving a greater sense of empowerment for service users and carers, as a result of intervention from social workers and occupational therapists. Part of the tension which is at work is that social workers and occupational therapists need to be prepared to loosen their control and embrace users' own definitions and solutions if the latter are to have an increased sense of empowerment, but those workers face constraining factors in the guise of their own organisation's priorities. Yet Tanner's work (Chapter Seven) indicates that attention is needed to *how* help is provided as well as to *what* help is provided:

> It is possible for help to address identified practical difficulties but to undermine the positive identity of the older person in the process of service delivery. This point brings together a number of issues raised earlier such as the need to attend and respond to the person's own definition of needs and requirements and the significance of delivering help through the medium of a personal and positive relationship. (p.129)

This highlights the significance of *how* the service is provided through professional–service user interaction and the room for manoeuvre which exists to build on this form of participation.

Barry (Chapter Eight) uses the example of Guardianship under the 1983 Mental Health Act to argue that the law can be used to benefit and empower service users. She starts from the premise that many social workers see Guardianship as working against social work principles of user empowerment, participation and partnership. She then challenges this through the use of two case studies and argues that the powers of a Guardianship Order can be used by the social worker to engage with the service user in an empowering way because a Community Order, as compared to compulsory admission to hospital, is consistent with the ethos of the least restrictive alternative in the Mental Health Act (1983). Barry cites in the case studies examples of work that could only have been undertaken in a community setting, through an order which facilitated engagement with service users.

Participation is, therefore, one of the key prospects to hold on to as social work moves in the direction of a greater emphasis on partnership. What are the possibilities for social work in the context of participation and partnership?

Possibilities

In future, service users are likely to have higher expectations of health and social services and to express their views more forcibly about the standard and quality of service delivery. There will be an increasing and pressing need to pool the total resources and allocate them on a more integrated basis, involving multi-disciplinary teams working in and through local access centres. Both managers and practitioners will have to give up their sectarian attitudes and defensive stances, which are all too common features of the present separate services. If health and social services are not to unite in statute, then they must be united in the same basic objectives.

So how might health and social services be provided in the next ten to twenty years? By that time I shall be entering old age and I envisage that my first point of contact for a service would be through the internet and an interactive discussion with a social worker about my needs and how they might be met. The local office will probably have disappeared some years ago, as an efficiency saving. The capital and revenue costs of running an office may have become so high as no longer to be economical. Most people now work from home with a communication network that is more efficient and rapid in response. So, having discussed my needs with the social worker who has treated me with dignity and respect, listened to my views, explained my rights and gone through the range of choices available to me, I will probably be able to view my care plan on the internet by using my personal identity number (PIN) for security access. I might then also be able to consider any implications for my health record maintained by my local GP and again accessible through the internet with my PIN number. My care plan would have been costed and authorised and my cash limit set for direct payment. I would now need to shop around for the best deal with providers, again using the internet. I would have to be wary of all the sales patter as I choose the ones to interrogate through my interactive button. The social worker has been really helpful with suggestions on the type of questions I need to ask and the quality of service I should be expecting. Still, if I have any problems I can seek further help from a consultation with my social worker.

Is this greater user participation through greater control of the resources and choices and how to utilise them? Is this real empowerment – being able to influence decisions and make informed decisions with further support, if required? It is the type of service that I would want to receive. I would want to feel that I am in charge or control and could organise services at my convenience in my own home. How is this service provided and by whom?

Social services as a stand-alone organisation changed some years ago. Care trusts now provide integrated health and social care for all adults, while children's services are linked to educational special needs and managed through regional government. Oversight of all these services is through a new national audit and inspection quango. Andrew Foster, controller of the Audit Commission, stated that the Audit Commission and Social Services Inspectorate joint reviews of the late 1990s and early 2000s had identified the key changes to be put in place with:

- a focus on outcomes for service users
- extension of existing partnership arrangements
- national guidance to deliver best value
- improved performance measurement
- strengthened project management. (Community Care 2001, p.6)

The care trusts have been able to build a form of organisation that broke down traditional barriers within health and social services in providing multi-disciplinary working. They also provided very valuable one-stop shops for the consumer, which prevented being passed between organisations with no one taking responsibility for the service outcomes.

Section 31 of the National Health Service Act (1999) has been fully implemented with the flexibility for different services paid for from pooled budgets and integrated provision. The local care trust provides a full service for older people with a pooled budget from both social services and the health authority. All of the resources available for the care needs of service users are combined into one budget and spent by one agency and in this imagined future it is the local care trust. The advantage of this is that it facilitates integrated packages of care for the older person. The social worker is able to access both health and social service budgets in the design of the care package. Since the pooled budget is with the care trust it comes within the regulations governing health which is a free service to the patient. Thus, the previous charges levied by social services have been phased out and the service for the older person is free of charge. The safeguard for the accountability of the service is that the managers of the care trust have to report back to social services committees on the outcomes of the use of the resource and this is, therefore, scrutinised by locally elected councillors.

In this future scenario lead commissioning enables the full commissioning of a service for a particular service user group by one organisation. For disability services for adults the social services was appointed as the lead commissioner. The service was the subject of a local authority best value review which led to the provision being located within the voluntary sector under a series of service level agreements for five-year periods with annual reviews. The service level agreements had a clear service specification with objectives, targets, outcomes, service user participation in managing the service, quality standards, monitoring reviews and an annual public appraisal report. The day centre for adults with a disability was set up as a co-operative with a management board consisting of a majority of disabled people. A national voluntary organisation is providing an assessment and resource centre working to national standards introduced by the government. When lead commissioning was introduced, there was an open tendering process for service delivery. Most staff chose to move to the successful provider after the tendering process, under their existing terms and conditions of service.

The most radical change under Section 31 of the National Health Service Act (1999) is integrated service delivery. In an integrated service, one organisation provides all of the services to a group of service users, irrespective of who has previously been the provider. The social services day centre for people with a learning disability now has integrated provision. Thus, the full range of services previously supplied by the social services and the health authority is located under one roof, the day centre. Nurses, psychologists, physiotherapists, occupational therapists and chiropodists are all employed by the social services department in addition to social workers and other social care staff. The skill mix within the centre means that different professionals are available when required and they work across several different centres on a sessional basis, in addition to providing home visits and support to carers.

In this section of the chapter I have tried to map out a range of the possibilities that might exist in a changing environment. I have tried to develop these ideas as opportunities for the social work profession rather than threats to its survival. Despite having often had hostile media coverage, social work has delivered much change over the years and the future holds out many possibilities for it to continue in this role. Social work will be located within a much more integrated partnership model of service delivery and it will involve a greater understanding of different professionals' perceptions and values. However, social work has much to offer to those other professionals through its historical development, its experience and its own value base and it will require those other professionals to change as well, as accommodations are made with respect to each other's contributions.

Conclusion

I began this chapter by stating that one of the certainties is that there is further change on the horizon for social work and community care. I then set out the context for further change as being the wide-scale developments of the late twentieth century. I argued that social work had proved itself to be capable of surviving and that while the changes in the future might seem daunting, they could be viewed as either a threat or an opportunity. I have put the case that the future holds an opportunity for social work if it can adapt, while holding on to its previous strengths. Prospects and possibilities intertwine; only when the prospects are clear is it feasible to determine the possibilities.

The previous chapters of the book draw on social work practice in Warwickshire. They highlight good practice. One of the strengths of good social work practice is its value base, rooted in close involvement and discussion with service users and carers, and active partnership with other professionals and agencies. Grass-roots service development, as represented in this book, is a key element for social work's future development. From collaboration to partnership, the social model versus the medical model, treating people as experts in their own problem-solving, managing imbalances of power – these are all components of grass-roots service development which hold out prospects for the future of social work.

If we get participation and partnership right in the future, the prospects are benefits for service users and carers. I have outlined some of the possible ways in which services might be delivered. All of these have the potential for a service where greater control is located with the service user, who is able to shape the delivery of her/his own care package. This has links with the overall vision in the NHS Plan, which is 'to create a service designed around the patient or user whilst recognising that this will require investment and reform' (Department of Health 2000a, p.17). If this is the way that the future unfolds, then the possibilities for both social work and better quality service provision in community care will be enhanced. Service users and their carers stand to benefit most from breaking down traditional barriers and a service that cannot pass the buck to others. The over-riding message from the chapters in this book is that to succeed any further reform needs to embrace the twin dimensions of partnership and participation.

An Example of a Discussion on Writing Good Assessments

Good assessment should refer to the views of service users and carers accurately and with due regard to confidentiality.

Problems

We identified some of the problems. For example:

- Doctors or nurses passing on a diagnosis to social workers, such as cancer, but saying the service user is not aware of it. Do we record it?
- Is it ethical to describe residential care in other ways? For example, 'Would you like to go somewhere to be looked after?'
- Carers may not want the service user to be aware of their feelings.
- Writing assessments in a positive way but so that the service user still gets the required resource.
- We are not always getting service users' signatures on the assessments.
- Are we reflecting and acknowledging what the service user really wants?
- We may attach nursing reports to our assessments that the service user has not seen.

Issues

We thought the issues behind these problems are:

- Asking questions too directly, such as, 'Do you want to go home?' 'Do you want to go into care?'
- We are not using service users' perceptions enough. They can often describe how they feel and what they want, but not in response to direct questions.

- We do not have to take others' judgements at face value. We can challenge why doctors have not disclosed a diagnosis. We can ask people if they would like to know their diagnosis.
- We need to ask doctors and nurses if they have discussed their reports with their patients.
- We can record in the confidential section if necessary, but service users can be sensitive to carers' needs.

Suggestions for recording

Carers

Mrs X is very fond of her mother, but on a bad day says she finds the need for constant reassurance very draining.

Expressed needs

Mrs X is very hesitant about going into a home and Mrs X says she would like to remain at home. I have discussed the risks with her, but she has little insight or awareness of the risks/cannot acknowledge the risks.

Health

Use 'becoming forgetful', 'is aware her memory is not good' or 'needs constant reminders'.

We should not use 'confusion', or 'dementia' without a diagnosis, or without explaining what it means. We can refer to specialist workers for more specific understanding of some people, and share decision-making.

Tips from the team

- Share decision-making.
- Share thoughts and useful phrases.
- BE HONEST with service users and carers about what we can and cannot do.
- Check with the service user what you are writing.
- Check with the service user: 'Are you worried about how you are feeling?' 'Do you want to know more from your doctor?'
- Always start by asking what the service user wants.
- Only record on a 'need to know' basis. Do not record unnecessary or intimate details.

APPENDIX TWO

In Assessment with Some Useful Phrases

Self-perceived needs and wishes

Mrs Yellow has cherished her independence and home very highly. Although she has begun to enjoy respite stays at The Beeches, she is always keen to return to her own home. Mrs Yellow has the capacity to make her own choices, but she does heed the advice of her daughter provided it does not threaten her own autonomy. However she does not have full insight into her needs for help, nor of the effects her difficulties have on her family.

Mrs Yellow is now becoming somewhat apprehensive at the prospect of the winter, the cold and the dark nights all on her own, and she, with the backing of her daughters and son, is asking if she could be considered for a permanent place at The Beeches. Mrs Yellow is a sociable but also very private person, so that her personal space, both physical and mental, needs to be approached with sensitivity and respect.

Self-care

Mrs Yellow lives on her own and washes and dresses herself independently, though her daughter does need to insist quite firmly on her changing her clothes which she takes away to wash. She does go upstairs to use the toilet, *though negotiating stairs is not easy for her.* There have been occasions when she has had an accident in or near to the toilet which she has difficulty in clearing up; the exact cause of these events is not known.

Mrs Yellow eats and drinks independently although she can no longer prepare meals nor shop for herself.

Mrs Yellow takes her medication herself, but is given just one day's supply in a Medidose pack which is delivered each morning, with due reminders to take it.

Health

Physical health

Mrs Yellow suffered from polio in her childhood and walks with a limp. Her reaction to her disability has been to be fiercely independent. She has long-standing anaemia. Mrs Yellow has had Parkinson's disease for several years, which causes unsteadiness early in the day, before her first medication has taken effect.

She has high blood pressure and cardiac problems, and suffers intermittently from Transient Ischaemic Attacks. Consequently she has had a number of brief hospital admissions in recent years. After the last attack in April an attempt was made to monitor her heart over 24 hours but Mrs Yellow was unable to adhere to the directions and took the monitor off.

Mental health

Mrs Yellow suffers from short-term memory loss, and she is very aware of this. These short-term memory losses cause her great frustration. Her long-term memory is good.

Mrs Yellow is sharp-thinking and articulate. She can be witty, but due to forgetfulness tends to be repetitive.

Mrs Yellow's health fluctuates quite markedly from day to day and from one time of day to another. *She only partially recognises her health problems* and consequent needs.

Medication

Thioridazine 10 mg. twice a day, morning and evening

Aspirin 75 mg., morning

Sinemet Plus, three times a day

Ferrous Sulphate, three times a day

Dipyridamole one capsule, morning and evening

Losec 10 mg., morning and evening.

Ideally Mrs Yellow should be given one day's supply of medication to take herself, with prompting if needed.

Informal network and support

Mrs Yellow's children are all extremely supportive of her, while her younger daughter Mrs Green is particularly involved on a day-to-day basis, doing shopping, bringing meals, doing washing and tactful cleaning when possible.

The demands on the family are particularly heavy because Mrs Yellow does not welcome other forms of outside help.

Service network

Community support workers visit every morning and bring the medication for the day. Meals-on-wheels and home care have been tried but did not meet with Mrs Yellow's approval and so have been discontinued.

Mrs Yellow is taken by a support worker to attend informal meetings at the Resource Centre, alternate Wednesdays 12.45pm–3.00pm and to a lunch club at the Centre on Fridays.

Community psychiatric nurses and social workers visit and make arrangements and referrals as needed.

Personal history

Mrs Yellow is well able to give her own story, and if a visitor displays knowledge of her background she will ask, 'How did you know that?' to which I can honestly reply, '*You* told me!' I shall write a brief personal history, which may help carers initially.

Mrs Yellow was born and grew up in Staffordshire, an only child who had a happy and secure childhood. She left school at 16 and trained in shorthand, typing and book-keeping. However when the family moved to [Warwickshire town] when she was 22 she worked as a printer. This was using die-casts to make raised printing such as that in raised letter-heads on superior stationery. She married at 26 and had three children, Sue, Philip and Helen, over 15 years and now has five grandchildren. Her husband was her closest companion over 50 years and they had a warm and happy home, always in the house where Mrs Yellow still lives. It was new when the Yellows moved into it on their marriage. Sadly Mr Yellow died about 13 years ago and since then Mrs Yellow has lived alone and independently until her health problems began to necessitate some help from her daughter Helen. Because Mrs Yellow so cherishes her own home her family have done their utmost to support her in her wish to stay there as long as possible.

Needs of carers

Mrs Yellow's family, especially her daughter Helen, need regular breaks from caring, especially as it is to her that Mrs Yellow turns constantly for help, rather than seeking or accepting care from other services. The endeavour has recently been to encourage Mrs Yellow to accept respite stays with a view to relieving Helen as well as maintaining her own well-being. However it does appear that the time is coming when respite care is insufficient to alleviate Helen's concerns for her mother, and strain upon herself.

It is also important that responsibility for the inevitable risks involved in Mrs Yellow remaining in her own home are shared between the family and the professional services.

Mobility

Mrs Yellow can walk short distances with a walking stick.

Risks

Mrs Yellow faces the following risks at home:

- risk of falling, especially when negotiating stairs
- risk of malnutrition due to forgetting to eat
- risk of self-neglect due to lack of awareness that she no longer carries out all the self-care tasks she used to do
- risk of forgetting to take medication
- risk of Transient Ischaemic Attacks and other untoward health events going unattended until discovered by someone.

Summary

Mrs Betty Yellow is an 88-year-old widow who has maintained her independence tenaciously and still lives in the house she moved into on marriage around 50 years ago. However she suffers from a number of health problems including short-term memory loss, *and does need considerable discreet assistance.* Mostly she depends on her daughter Helen, with some support from her other children, and from community support services. Mrs Yellow has not been happy with home care or meals-on-wheels services, so these have been discontinued.

Mrs Yellow has had three periods of respite at The Beeches, these have gone very well. Mrs Yellow has also been attending day care twice a week for the past few months.

References

Adams, R. (1996) *Social Work and Empowerment*. Basingstoke: Macmillan.

Ahmad, W.I.U. and Atkin, K. (1996) *'Race' and Community Care*. Buckingham: Open University Press.

Atkin, K. (1991) 'Community care in multi-racial society: incorporating the user view.' *Policy and Politics 19*, 3, 159–166.

Atkin, K. and Rollings, J. (1993) *Community Care in a Multi-racial Britain: A Critical Review of the Literature*. London: HMSO.

Audit Commission (1983) *Handbook on Economy, Efficiency and Effectiveness*. London: HMSO.

Audit Commission (1986) *Making a Reality of Community Care*. London: HMSO.

Audit Commission (1988) *The Competitive Council*. London: HMSO.

Audit Commission (1992a) *The Community Revolution: The Personal Social Services and Community Care*. London: HMSO.

Audit Commission (1992b) *Homeward Bound: A New Course for Community Health*. London: HMSO.

Audit Commission (1997) *The Coming of Age: Improving Care Services for Older People*. London: HMSO.

Audit Commission (2000) *Forget Me Not: Mental Health Services for Older People*. London: HMSO.

Baldock, J. (1993) 'Patterns of change in the delivery of welfare in Europe.' In P. Taylor-Gooby and R. Lawson (eds) *Markets and Managers. New Issues in the Delivery of Welfare*. Buckingham: Open University Press.

Baldock, J. (1998) 'Old age, consumerism and the social care market.' In E. Brunsden, H. Dean and R. Woods (eds) *Social Policy Review 10*. London: Social Policy Association.

Baldock, J. and Ungerson, C. (1994) *Becoming Consumers of Community Care: Households within the Mixed Economy of Welfare*. York: Joseph Rowntree Foundation.

Baldwin, M. (1996) 'Is assessment working? Policy and practice in care management.' *Practice 8*, 4, 53–59.

Baldwin, M. (2000) *Care Management and Community Care: Social Work Discretion and the Construction of Policy*. Aldershot: Ashgate.

Baldwin, N., Harris, J., Littlechild, R. and Pearson, M. (1993) *Residents' Rights: A Strategy in Action in Homes for Older People*. Aldershot: Avebury.

Banks, S. (1995) *Ethics and Values in Social Work*. Basingstoke: Macmillan.

Barnes, M. (1997) *Care, Communities and Citizens*. Harlow: Longman.

Barnes, M. and Prior, D. (1996) 'From private choice to public trust: a new social basis for welfare.' *Public Money and Management 16*, 17–26.

Barnes, M. and Walker, A. (1998) 'Principles of empowerment.' In M. Allot and M. Robb (eds) (1998) *Understanding Health and Social Care*. London: Sage.

Barnes, M. and Wistow, G. (1994) 'Achieving a strategy for user involvement in community care.' *Health and Social Care in the Community 2*, 34–56.

Bartlett, H. (1999) 'Primary health care for older people: progress towards an integrated strategy?' *Health and Social Care in the Community 7*, 5, 342–349.

Bennett, G., Kingston, P. and Penhale, B. (1997) *The Dimensions of Elder Abuse*. Basingstoke: Macmillan.

Beresford, P. and Croft, S. (1993) *Citizen Involvement: A Practical Guide for Change*. Basingstoke: Macmillan.

Beresford, P., Croft, S., Evans, C. and Harding, T. (1997) 'Quality in personal social services: the developing role of user involvement in the UK.' In A. Evers, R. Haverinen, K. Leischenring and G. Wistow (eds) *Developing Quality in Personal Social Services: Concepts, Cases and Comments*. Aldershot: Ashgate.

Beresford, P. and Turner, M. (1997) *It's Our Welfare: Report of the Citizen's Commission on the Future of Welfare*. London: National Institute for Social Work.

Biehal, N., Fisher, M. and Sainsbury, E. (1992) 'Rights and social work.' In A. Coote (ed) *The Welfare of Citizens*. London: Rivers Oram Press.

Biggs, S. (1997) 'User voice, interprofessionalism and postmodernity.' *Journal of Interprofessional Care 11*, 2, 195–203.

Blakemore, K. and Boneham, M. (1994) *Age, Race and Ethnicity. A Comparative Approach*. Buckingham: Open University Press.

Braye, S. and Preston-Shoot, M. (1995) *Empowering Practice in Social Care.* Buckingham: Open University Press.

Braye, S. and Preston-Shoot, M. (1998) 'Social work and the law'. In R. Adams, L. Dominelli and M. Payne (eds) *Social Work. Themes, Issues and Critical Debates.* Basingstoke: Macmillan.

Burton, D. (2000) 'REACT: an evaluation of the first 15 months.' *Nurse-2-Nurse.* March.

Bury, M. (1991) 'The sociology of chronic illness: a review of research and prospects.' *Sociology of Health and Illness 13,* 4, 451–468.

Butler Report (1975) *Report of the Committee on Mentally Abnormal Offenders.* London: HMSO.

Butt, J. (1994) *Same Service or Equal Service?* London: HMSO.

Bywaters, P. and McLeod, E. (eds) (1996) *Working for Equality in Health.* London: Routledge.

Cabinet Office (1999) *Modernising Government.* London: HMSO.

Carpenter, M. (1994) *Normality is Hard Work: Trade Unions and the Politics of Community Care.* London: Lawrence and Wishart.

Cattell, H. (1994) 'Suicidal behaviour.' In J.R.M. Copeland, M.T. Abou-Saleh and D.G. Blazer (eds) *Principles and Practice of Geriatric Psychiatry.* Chichester: John Wiley.

CCETSW (1992) *Contracting and Case Management in Community Care. The Challenges for Local Authorities.* London: CCETSW.

CCETSW (1994) *Purchasing and Contracting Skills.* London: CCETSW.

CCETSW (1998) *Assuring Quality for Practice Teaching.* London: CCETSW.

Charmaz, K. (1983) 'Loss of self: a fundamental form of suffering in the chronically ill.' *Sociology of Health and Illness 5,* 2, 168–195.

Clark, H., Dyer, S. and Horwood, J. (1998) *That Bit of Help: The High Value of Low Level Preventative Services for Older People.* Bristol: Policy Press.

Clarke, J. (1996) 'After social work?' In N. Parton (ed) *Social Theory, Social Change and Social Work.* London: Routledge.

Clarke, J., Cochrane, A. and McLaughlin, E. (eds) (1994) *Managing Social Policy.* London: Sage.

Clarke, J. and Newman, J. (1997) *The Managerial State.* London: Sage.

Coleman, P., Ivani-Chalian, C. and Robinson, M. (1998) 'The story continues: persistence of life themes in old age.' *Ageing and Society 18,* 389–419.

Community Care (2000) *News Item,* 9 January, pp.20–21.

Community Care (2001) *News Item.* 4 February, p.6.

Connolly, J. (1997) 'The hospital.' In M. Davies (ed) *The Blackwell Companion to Social Work.* Oxford: Blackwell.

Connor, A. and Tibbitt, J.E. (1988) *Social Workers and Health Care in Hospitals.* Edinburgh: HMSO.

Coulshed, V. and Orme, J. (1998) *Social Work Practice. An Introduction.* Basingstoke: Macmillan.

Dalrymple, J. and Burke, B. (1995) *Anti-oppressive Practice: Social Care and the Law.* Buckingham: Open University Press.

Davis, A., Ellis, K. and Rummery, K. (1997) *Access to Assessment: Perspectives of Practitioners, Disabled People and Carers.* Bristol: Policy Press.

Department of Health (1989) *Caring for People: Community Care in the Next Decade and Beyond.* London: HMSO.

Department of Health (1990a) *Community Care in the Next Decade and Beyond: Policy Guidance.* London: HMSO.

Department of Health (1990b) *The Care Programme Approach for People with a Mental Illness Referred to the Specialist Psychiatric Services.* Joint Health/Social Services Circular, HC(90), 23/LASS, (90) 11. London: HMSO.

Department of Health (1994a) *A Framework for Local Care Charters in England.* London: HMSO.

Department of Health (1994b) *Hospital Discharge Workbook.* London: HMSO.

Department of Health (1995) *Building Bridges: A Guide to Arrangements for Inter-agency Working for the Care and Protection of Severely Mentally Ill People.* London: HMSO.

Department of Health (1997a) *Better Services for Vulnerable People.* London: HMSO.

Department of Health (1997b) *The New National Health Service: Modern, Dependable.* London: HMSO.

Department of Health (1997c) *Guardianship under the Mental Health Act (1983).* London: HMSO.

Department of Health (1998a) *Modernising Social Services.* London: HMSO.

Department of Health (1998b) *Partnership in Action. New Opportunities for Joint Working Between Health and Social Services.* London: HMSO.

Department of Health (1998c) *Better Health and Better Health Care: Implementing the New NHS and Our Healthier Nation.* London: HMSO.

Department of Health (1998d) *National Priorities Guidance.* London: HMSO.

Department of Health (1998e) *Statistical Bulletin: In-patients Detained in Hospitals Under the Mental Health Act 1983 and Other Legislation in England 1987–1988; 1992–1993; 1997–1998.* London: HMSO.

Department of Health (1999a) *Saving Lives: Our Healthier Nation.* London: HMSO.

Department of Health (1999b) *Review of the Mental Health Act (1983).* London: HMSO.

Department of Health (1999c) *National Strategy for Carers.* London: HMSO.

Department of Health (1999d) *Mental Health Act. Memorandum on Parts I to VI, VIII and X.* London: HMSO.

Department of Health (1999e) *Mental Health Act. Code of Practice.* London: HMSO.

Department of Health (2000a) *The NHS Plan.* London: HMSO.

Department of Health (2000b) *Modernising Mental Health.* London: HMSO.

Department of Health (2000c) *Community Care Statistics 1999: Home Help/Home Care Services in England.* London: HMSO.

Department of Health (2000d) *A Quality Strategy for Social Care.* London: HMSO.

Department of Health (2001a) *Reforming the Mental Health Act. The New Legal Framework.* London: HMSO.

Department of Health (2001b) *The NHS Plan. Implementing the Performance Improvement Agenda.* London: NHS Executive.

Dooher, L. (1989) 'Research note: guardianship under the Mental Health Act 1983. Practice in Leicestershire.' *British Journal of Social Work 19,* 129–135.

Dube, R. (1997) *The Care Programme Approach: Key Issues for CPNs.* CPA Publications, North Birmingham Health Authority.

Dyer, C. (1987) 'Compulsory treatment in the community for the mentally ill?' *British Medical Journal 295,* 991–992.

Eaton, L. (2000) 'Time is not always money.' *Community Care.* 21–27 September, 22–23.

Ellis, K. (1993) *Squaring the Circle: User and Carer Participation in Needs Assessment and Community Care.* York: Joseph Rowntree Foundation.

Farnham, D. and Horton, S. (eds) (1993) *Managing the New Public Services.* Basingstoke: Macmillan.

Finch, J. and Mason, J. (1993) *Negotiating Family Responsibilities.* London: Routledge.

Fisk, M. and Abbott, S. (1998) 'Older people and the meaning of independence.' *Generations Review 8,* 2, 9–11.

Fletcher, P. (1998) 'Focus on prevention: back on the political agenda.' *Working with Older People 2,* 3, 8–12.

Flynn, N. (1993, second edition) *Public Sector Management.* London: Harvester Wheatsheaf.

Gearing, B. and Dant, T. (1990) 'Doing biographical research.' In S. Peace (ed) *Researching Social Gerontology: Concepts, Methods and Issues.* London: Sage.

Gelles, R. and Strauss, M.A. (1979) 'Violence in America.' *Journal of Social Issues 35,* 15–39.

Goodwin, J. (1999) *Reform of the Mental Health Act 1983. Summary of Proposals for Consultation.* Birmingham: North Birmingham Health Trust.

Gostin, L. (1975) *A Human Condition – Vol 1.* London: Mind Publications.

Graham, A. (1990) 'Guardianship post of caring' *Community Care,* February 1990.

Griffiths Report (1988) *Community Care: An Agenda for Action.* London: HMSO.

Harding, T. and Beresford, P. (1996) *The Standards We Expect: What Service Users and Carers Want from Social Services Workers.* London: National Institute of Social Work.

Harris, J. (1998a) 'Scientific management, bureau-professionalism and new managerialism. The labour process of state social work.' *British Journal of Social Work 28,* 839–862.

Harris, J. (1998b) *Managing State Social Work.* Aldershot: Ashgate.

Harris, J. (1999) 'State social work and social citizenship in Britain: from clientelism to consumerism.' *British Journal of Social Work 29,* 915–937.

Harris, J. and McDonald, C. (2000) 'Post-Fordism, the welfare state and the personal social services. A comparison of Australia and Britain.' *British Journal of Social Work 30,* 51–70.

Haslam, M. (1990) *Psychiatry.* Oxford: Butterworth Heinemann.

Henwood, M. (1992) *Through a Glass Darkly.* London: Kings Fund.

Henwood, M., Lewis, H. and Waddington, E. (1998) 'I'll tell you what I want.' *Community Care.* 22–28 January, 28–29.

Hepinstall, D. (1992) 'Home truths?' *Community Care.* 30 July, 25–26.

Hoggett, P. (1991) 'A new management in the public sector?' *Policy and Politics 19,* 243–256.

Holstein, J. and Gubrium, J. (1997) 'Active interviewing.' In D. Silverman (ed) *Qualitative Research: Theory, Method and Practice*. London: Sage.

House of Commons Social Services Committee (1985) *Community Care*. London: HMSO.

Hughes, G. (1990) 'Trends in Guardianship usage following the Mental Health Act 1983.' *Health Trends 22*, 145–147.

Hughes, R.D. and Bhaduri, R. (1987) *Social Services for Ethnic Minorities*. Manchester: Social Services Inspectorate NW Region.

Huntington, J. (1986) 'The proper contribution of social workers in health practice.' *Social Science and Medicine 22*, 11, 1151–1160.

Husband, C. (1996) 'Defining and containing diversity: community, ethnicity and citizenship.' In W.I.U. Ahmad and K. Atkin (eds) *'Race' and Community Care*. Buckingham: Open University Press.

Irish, M. (1988) 'Guardianship and the elderly: a multi-perspective view of the decision-making process.' *The Gerontologist, 28*, 39–45.

Jones, C. (1994, second edition) *The Making of Social Policy in Britain, 1830–1990*. London: Athlone Press.

Jones, R. (1999) *Mental Health Act Manual*. London: Sweet and Maxwell.

Labour Party (1991) *Citizen's Charter: Labour's Better Deal for Consumers and Citizens*. London: The Labour Party.

Laffin, M. and Young, K. (1990) *Professionalism in Local Government*. Harlow: Longman.

Langan, J., Means, R. and Rolfe, S. (1996) *Maintaining Independence in Later Life: Older People Speaking*. Oxford: Anchor Trust.

Langan, M. (1993) 'New directions in social work.' In J. Clarke (ed) *A Crisis in Care? Challenges to Social Work*. London: Sage.

Langan, M. (2000) 'Social services: managing the Third Way.' In J. Clarke, S. Gewirtz and E. McLaughlin (eds) *New Managerialism, New Welfare?* London: Sage.

Langan, M. and Clarke, J. (1994) 'Managing in the mixed economy of care.' In J. Clarke, A. Cochrane and E. McLaughlin (eds) *Managing Social Policy*. London: Sage.

Le Grand, J. (1990) *Quasi-markets and Social Policy. Studies in Decentralisation and Quasi-markets No. 1*. Bristol: School for Advanced Urban Studies, University of Bristol.

Le Grand, J. (1993) *Quasi-Markets*. Basingstoke: Macmillan.

Le Grand, J. and Robinson, R. (1984) (eds) *Privatisation and the Welfare State*. London: Unwin Hyman.

Lewis, H., Fletcher, P., Hardy, B., Milne, A. and Waddington, E. (1999) *Promoting Well-being: Developing a Preventative Approach with Older People*. Oxford: Anchor Trust.

Lewis, J. and Glennerster, H. (1996) *Implementing the New Community Care*. Buckingham: Open University Press.

Lindesay, I., Briggs, K. and Murphy, E. (1989) 'The Guys/Age Concern Survey: prevalence rates of cognitive impairment, depression and anxiety in an urban elderly community.' *British Journal of Psychiatry 155*, 317–329.

Local Government Training Board (1985) *Good Management in Local Government. Successful Practice and Action*. Luton: Local Government Training Board.

Manning, G.M. (1988) 'Time for clarification.' *Social Work Today*. 17 November, 17–19.

Marsh, P. (1998) 'Task-centered work.' In M. Davies (ed) *The Blackwell Companion to Social Work*. Oxford: Blackwell.

Marsh, P. and Fisher, M. (1992) *Good Intentions: Developing Partnership in Social Services*. York: Joseph Rowntree Foundation.

Marshall, M. and Dixon, M. (1996) *Social Work with Older People*. Basingstoke: Macmillan.

Mason, D. (1997) *The Future of Social Services*. Warwick: Warwickshire County Council.

McDonald, A. and Taylor, M. (1995) *The Law and Elderly People*. London: Sweet and Maxwell.

McLeod, E. and Bywaters, P. (2000) *Social Work, Health and Equality*. London: Routledge.

Mental Health Act Commission (1983–1985) *First Biennial Report*. London: HMSO.

Mental Health Act Commission (1985–1987) *Second Biennial Report*. London: HMSO.

Mental Health Act Commission (1987–1989) *Third Biennial Report*. London: HMSO.

Mental Health Act Commission (1989–1991) *Fourth Biennial Report*. London: HMSO.

Mental Health Act Commission (1991–1993) *Fifth Biennial Report*. London: HMSO.

Mental Health Act Commission (1993–1995) *Sixth Biennial Report*. London: HMSO.

Millington, S. (1989) *Guardianship and the Mental Health Act (1983)*. Norwich: University of East Anglia, Social Work Monographs.

Milner, J. and O'Byrne, P. (1998) *Assessment in Social Work*. Basingstoke: Macmillan.

Minichiello, V., Browne, J. and Kendig, H. (2000) 'Perceptions and consequences of ageism: views of older people.' *Ageing and Society 30*, 3, 253–278.

Morris, J. (1993) *Independent Lives? Community Care and Disabled People.* Basingstoke: Macmillan.

Morris, J. (1996) *Encounter with Strangers: Feminism and Disability.* London: Women's Press.

Mullender, A. and Ward, D. (1991) *Self Directed Groupwork: Users Take Action for Empowerment.* London: Whiting and Birch.

Myers, F. and MacDonald, C. (1996) 'I was given options not choices: involving older users and carers in assessment and care planning.' In R. Bland (ed) *Developing Services for Older People and their Families.* London: Jessica Kingsley Publishers.

National Institute for Social Work (1990) *Black Community and Community Care.* London: Race Equality Unit, NISW.

Oldman, C. (1991) *Paying for Care: Personal Sources of Funding Care.* York: Joseph Rowntree Foundation.

Pakulski, J. (1997) 'Cultural citizenship.' *Citizenship Studies 1*, 73–86.

Papadakis, E. and Taylor-Gooby, P. (1987) *The Private Provision of Public Welfare. State, Market and Community.* Brighton: Wheatsheaf.

Parker, H. (ed) (2000) *Low Cost but Acceptable Incomes for Older People: A Minimum Income Standard for Households Aged 65–74 Years in the UK.* Bristol: The Policy Press.

Parton, N. and O'Byrne, P. (2000) *Constructive Social Work. Towards a New Practice.* Basingstoke: Macmillan.

Patel, N. (1990) *A 'Race' Against Time?* London: The Runnymede Trust.

Patmore, C., Qureshi, H. and Nicholas, E. (1999) 'Tuning in to feedback.' *Community Care.* 24–30 June, 28–29.

Payne, M. (1995) *Social Work and Community Care.* Basingstoke: Macmillan.

Payne, M. (1996) 'Government guidance in the construction of the social work profession.' Paper presented at Crisis in the Human Services Conference, University of Cambridge.

Phillipson, C. (1992) 'Interprofessional collaboration: problems and prospects for the 1990s.' *Journal of Professional Care 16*, 1, 7–16.

Pierson, C. (1991) *Beyond the Welfare State? The New Political Economy of Welfare.* Cambridge: Polity Press.

Pollitt, C. (1990) *Managerialism and the Public Services.* Oxford: Blackwell.

Pratt, M. and Norris, J. (1994) *The Social Psychology of Ageing.* Oxford: Blackwell.

Prime Minister (1991) *The Citizen's Charter: Raising the Standard.* London: HMSO.

Quilgars, D. (2000) *Low Intensity Support Services: A Systematic Review of Effectiveness.* Bristol: The Policy Press.

R. v. Kent County Council *ex parte* (1997) *Queen's Bench Division*, 9 July.

Richards, S. (2000) 'Bridging the divide: elders and the assessment process.' *British Journal of Social Work 30*, 37–49.

Richardson, S. and Pearson, M. (1995) 'Dignity and aspirations denied: unmet health and social care needs in an inner-city area.' *Health and Social Care in the Community 3*, 5 279–287.

Robbins, I. (1994) 'The long-term consequences of war trauma: a review and case example.' *PSIGE Newsletter 48*, 2–28.

Royal Commission (1999) *Report on Long-term Care.* London: HMSO.

Schwehr, B. (1999) *Local Authority Rationing in the Provision of Services.* London: Rowe and Maw.

Scott, A. and Wenger, C. (1995) 'Gender and social support networks in later life.' In S. Arber and J. Ginn (eds) *Connecting Gender and Ageing: A Sociological Approach.* Buckingham: Open University Press.

Seebohm Report (1968) *Report of the Committee on Local Authority and Allied Personal Social Services.* London: HMSO.

Seed, P. and Kaye, G. (1994) *Handbook for Assessing and Managing Care in the Community.* London: Jessica Kingsley Publishers.

Smale, G. and Tuson, G. (1993) *Empowerment, Assessment, Care Management and the Skilled Worker.* London: HMSO.

Smale, G., Tuson, G. and Statham, D. (2000) *Social Work and Social Problems: Working Towards Social Inclusion and Social Change.* Basingstoke: Macmillan.

Social Services Inspectorate (1991a) *Care Management and Assessment: Practitioners' Guide.* London: HMSO.

Social Services Inspectorate (1991b) *Care Management and Assessment: Managers' Guide.* London: HMSO.

Social Services Inspectorate (1998) *Getting Better? Inspection of Hospital Discharge (Care Management) Arrangements for Older People.* London: HMSO.

Stanley, N. (1999) 'User–practitioner transactions in the new culture of community care.' *British Journal of Social Work 29*, 417–435.

Stevenson, O. and Parsloe, P. (1993) *Community Care and Empowerment.* York: Joseph Rowntree Foundation.

Strauss, A. and Corbin, J. (1998) 'Grounded theory methodology: an overview.' In N. Denzin and Y. Lincoln (eds) *Strategies of Qualitative Inquiry.* London: Sage.

Tanner, D. (1998) 'Empowerment and care management: swimming against the tide.' *Health and Social Care in the Community 6*, 6, 447–457.

Taylor-Gooby, P. (1987) 'Welfare attitudes: cleavage, consensus and citizenship.' *Quarterly Journal of Social Affairs 3*, 199–211.

Thompson, N. (1997, second edition) *Anti-discriminatory Practice.* Basingstoke: Macmillan.

Thompson, N. (1998) 'Social work with adults.' In R. Adams, L. Dominelli and M. Payne (eds) *Social Work Themes, Issues and Critical Debates.* Basingstoke: Macmillan.

Thompson, N. (2000) *Understanding Social Work.* Basingstoke: Macmillan.

Thompson, P., Itzin, C. and Abendstern, M. (1990) *I Don't Feel Old: The Experience of Later Life.* Oxford: Oxford University Press.

Thornton, P. and Tozer, R. (1994) *Involving Older People in Planning and Evaluating Community Care: A Review of Initiatives.* York: Joseph Rowntree Foundation.

Tulle-Winton, E. (1999) 'Growing old and resistance: towards a new cultural economy of old age?' *Ageing and Society 19*, 281–299.

Twigg, J. (1997) 'Deconstructing the "social bath": help with bathing at home for older and disabled people.' *Journal of Social Policy 26*, 2, 211–232.

Vernon, S. (1990) *Social Work and the Law.* London: Butterworth.

Wagner Report (1988) *Residential Care. A Positive Choice.* London: HMSO.

Walker, A. (1997) 'Community care policy: from consensus to conflict.' In J. Bornat, C. Johnson, C. Pereira, D. Pilgrim and F. Williams (eds) *Community Care: A Reader.* Basingstoke: Macmillan.

Walker, R. and Ahmad, W.I.U. (1994) 'Windows of opportunity in rotting frames: care providers' perspectives on community care and black communities.' *Critical Social Policy 40*, 46–69.

Warwickshire County Council (2000) *Our County. Warwickshire County Council Plan.* Warwick: Warwickshire County Council.

Warwickshire Social Services Department (1996) *Community Care: Practice Guidance.* Warwick: Warwickshire County Council.

Warwickshire Social Services Department (1998) *Guardianship Procedures.* Warwick: Warwickshire County Council.

Warwickshire Social Services Department (2000) *Joint Agency Community Care Plan.* Warwick: Warwickshire County Council.

Watson, P. (1996) 'Guardianship.' *Open Mind.* December/January, 13–15.

Watt, S. and Cook, J. (1989) 'Another expectation unfulfilled: Black women and Social Services Departments.' In C. Hallett (ed) *Women and Social Services Departments.* Hemel Hempstead: Harvester Wheatsheaf.

Watters, C. (1995) 'Representations of Asians in British psychiatry.' In C. Samson and N. South (eds) *Social Construction of Social Policy.* Basingstoke: Macmillan.

Wenger, G.C. (1984) *The Supportive Network: Coping with Old Age.* London: George Allen and Unwin.

White, V. (1999) 'Feminist social work and the state: a British perspective.' In B. Lešnick (ed) *Social Work and the State. International Perspectives in Social Work.* Brighton: Pavilion Press.

White, V. and Harris, J. (1999) 'Social Europe, social citizenship and social work.' *European Journal of Social Work 2*, 3–14.

White Paper (1989) *Caring for People: Into the Next Decade and Beyond.* London: HMSO.

Wilkin, D. (1990) 'Dependency.' In S. Peace (ed) *Researching Social Gerontology: Concepts, Methods and Issues.* London: Sage.

Wilson, G. (1993) 'Money and independence in old age.' In S. Arber and M. Evandrou (eds) *Ageing, Independence and the Life Course.* London: Jessica Kingsley Publishers.

Winchester, R. (2001) 'Compulsion fears stall support for White Paper.' *Community Care.* 11–17 January, 10–11.

Wistow, G., Callaghan, J., Randall, T. and Waddington, E. (2001) *First Steps in Prevention: Review of the 1999–2000 Prevention Plans.* Leeds: Nuffield Institute for Health.

Wistow, G. and Lewis, H. (1997) *Preventative Services for Older People: Current Approaches and Future Opportunities.* Oxford: Anchor Trust.

Contributors

Nicolette Barry is a senior social worker in a newly established mental health assertive outreach team in Birmingham Social Services Department. Her contribution to the book was undertaken when she was a social worker in a community care team providing services for adults in Warwickshire Social Services Department.

Linda Fleming has been a senior social worker in a community care team providing services for adults, for the last four years. From 1983 until taking up her present post she was a social worker.

Chris Hallett is a district manager. He held a variety of social work posts in generic settings before moving into management as a principal social worker, and then becoming a team manager. He has also been a quality assurance officer and the manager responsible for staff development.

John Harris is a reader in the School of Health and Social Studies, University of Warwick. He worked previously as a generic social worker, training officer and district manager in a social services department. He was granted a period of leave by the university to work as a social worker in a community care team providing services for adults in Warwickshire Social Services Department. This experience led on to the project on which the book is based.

Mehrunnisa Lalani is an equality advisor with Derby City Council. She worked previously in Warwickshire Social Services Department on the development of services to minority ethnic groups. Her varied career has included work in the voluntary sector and the health service, as well as managing a mental health service in a social services department.

Carole McSparran has worked in a community care team providing services for adults since qualifying as a social worker. At the time of writing, she is a temporary senior social worker.

Jez Millen is a senior social worker responsible for a unit of social work and administrative staff providing assessment and care management services to older people and people with learning disabilities. He has worked previously as a social worker in both a community mental health team for older people and a community care team providing services for adults.

Ann Morrison has been a team manager in a community care team providing services for adults for ten years. Previously she worked in the statutory and voluntary sectors, as a practitioner and as a project development worker.

Carol Roy is a senior hospital social worker. Prior to entering social work, she had a career as a general nurse. She has worked as a senior social worker in a community learning disabilities team.

Denise Tanner is a lecturer in social work at Coventry University. She was formerly a social worker and senior social worker with Warwickshire Social Services Department.

Lesley Wallman-Durrant is a community psychiatric nurse who has worked in a multi-disciplinary community mental health team for older people since 1993. Prior to this, she managed an assessment unit for older people and has worked in a variety of settings with people experiencing mental health problems across the age range.

Barbara Walters is team manager in a community care team providing services for adults, covering a large, mainly rural, geographical area. Her previous experience includes several years as a hospital social worker.

Eileen Watts was a senior social worker in a health-related team providing services for adults until her recent retirement. She had a varied career in social work with children and adults.

Vicky White is a lecturer in the School of Health and Social Studies, University of Warwick. She has worked as a generic social worker, a hospital social worker, a residential social worker and in a family placement unit.

Jon Whiting is a service manager (adult). He worked previously as a social worker, team manager and development manager (services for older people).

Subject Index

Name Index